Life through the Lens of Unschooling

A Living Joyfully Companion

PAM LARICCHIA

Published by
Living Joyfully Enterprises
Erin, Ontario, Canada

ISBN: 978-0-9877333-7-5

Edited by Alexandra Peace.

Cover design by Jane Dixon-Smith.

"One's mind, once stretched by a new idea,
never regains its original dimensions."

Oliver Wendell Holmes, Sr.

contents

chapter four: parenting

Let's talk about the kind of parenting that supports unschooling.

chapter five: relationships

What do relationships look like through the lens of unschooling?

chapter six: family

Looking at unschooling from the perspective of the family.

chapter seven: lifestyle
Musings on unschooling as a lifestyle.

chapter eight: unconventional
Unschooling is decidedly unconventional.

chapter nine: perspective
Some of the ways my perspective on things has grown through unschooling.

appendix

thank you!

acknowledgments

about Pam Laricchia

introduction

When I first started blogging regularly about unschooling in the fall of 2012, it was a place for me to have some fun. I had one book published at that point, *Free to Learn: Five Ideas for a Joyful Unschooling Life*, which I had written with an eye to being concise, accessible, and as helpful as possible for people trying to understand the principles behind unschooling. The blog was, and is, a place I could share more about the day-to-day antics of living with unschooling. Share some personal experiences. What does life look like for an unschooling family? And I could ask myself questions and play with the answers in short bursts, without the need to form a larger narrative.

Now we're in early 2014 and the Living Joyfully with Unschooling blog has over sixty posts of varying length, covering a wide array of topics that look at life through the lens of unschooling. Yet the chronological nature of an online blog means that, for the reader, it's easy to find the most recent posts, but even with categorizing and tagging, digging through the inventory to find the particular posts that would be most helpful to them at this particular moment of their unschooling journey is challenging.

I began to think about the value of bringing together all this writing in a more manageable format. Yet I also didn't want to just create a "blog in a book form." The chronological nature of the writing is now irrelevant. And the posts are already categorized by monthly topic on the blog, so that's taken care of. How might I bring this project together so that it has greater value for the reader?

So I created a swirling pot of *all* the posts. I stirred and peeked and stirred some more. I played with numerous ways to organize and group them, looking for ways that might bring additional clarity beyond the posts themselves. Eventually I hit upon the single words you see in the table of contents. These are words that, since we began unschooling in 2002, have been woven into the fabric of my understanding of unschooling. And as I sorted and re-sorted my blog posts into these threads, some wonderful synergies emerged.

You may find some content overlap, yet each time it's within a different context. I specifically chose to keep that because I don't know which context will make sense for which readers. That's how learning works—different connections for different people.

Gathering my blog writing into book form also gave me the perfect excuse to work with my lovely editor again! Typos were caught, thoughts clarified, grammar tightened. All very good things.

Why call it a companion?

I've chosen to call it a companion book because it's not meant to explain the ABCs of unschooling. It doesn't march from beginning to end, illuminating different aspects of a single theme. It meanders here and there, diving into the thoughts and questions I have pondered on the blog up to this point in time. The theme is life; the lens— unschooling. I imagine it accompanying you, a joyful companion on your unschooling journey, as you dig deeper into your understanding of unschooling and what it might look like day-to-day in your family.

Speaking of which, it needn't be read in order. If you're wondering about something in particular, skim through the table of contents. Which word seems most closely related? Which post seems like it might stretch your thinking, or spark new insights?

Thank you for inviting me along on your unschooling journey!

CHAPTER ONE

:: deschooling ::

Some ideas to consider as you begin your journey to unschooling.

Why Deschooling?

Deschooling is a general term used to describe the transition period as we shift from school or school-at-home to unschooling. For children, it's about rediscovering life outside the walls of the classroom, and the confines of a daily schedule dictated by the clock. For parents, it's a time when we explore and expand our definition of learning beyond the classroom paradigm. Conventional wisdom has told us that learning looks like teachers and listening and writing and tests. And even years after we've graduated, chances are our vision of learning is still locked within those four walls. But what might we see if we remove our school goggles?

The guideline surrounding deschooling is that the process typically takes about one month per year of school or school-at-home. Right away that tells us that parents will likely have the bulk of the work to do—which makes sense because we've been enmeshed in school culture the longest. Really, it takes as long as it takes, but where the statement really helps is planting the idea that the process takes a while. Not a few weeks or a couple months, but some real time. Long enough that when you're nearing the end, hopefully you've reached the point where you're not even looking for "the end" any more.

That's a great point to remember when you find yourself feeling overwhelmed with information and begin to worry: deschooling is going to take months and months. And months. I recall posting on a homeschooling forum about six weeks after my children left school about my worry that, at least my older two (ages 10 and 8 at the time), just wanted to play all the time. I was encouraged to relax and I think someone mentioned the longer time line of deschooling at that point. I relaxed and six months or so down the road I looked back at that post and laughed, realizing how tightly I had been clinging to my school goggles—I wasn't yet seeing all the learning that was happening in their play.

Moving to unschooling is a process. Six weeks can seem like a long time when you feel like you've leaped into the unknown, but in the grand scheme of things, it's just a blip on the radar. If you find yourself questioning your choices, that's good! It's part of the process. Do your best to answer your questions; don't just throw up your hands in defeat. And yet be careful not to use the longer-term nature of deschooling as an excuse to dilly-dally: take another step forward, and another. Keep learning and observing and thinking. You can't change past moments, but right here, right now, is a new moment in which you get to choose how to act and react.

For me, it was probably about a year before I felt like we were truly unschooling, not deschooling. There was no announcement, no graduation ceremony, but one day I realized I no longer felt like I was emulating the lifestyle—we were living it. I was no longer trying to wrap my mind around the principles; instead I was spending my time supporting how those principles were playing out in my unique family.

So how do you get there?

Something spurred you to investigate unschooling and whatever it was, that's a great place to start because that's where unschooling has made a connection with you. What conventional idea were you questioning? What unschooling action or principle caught your attention in response? Why? If you stay with the conventional wisdom, how might it play out in your family over the next five years? What about the unschooling perspective? What might that look like in your family today? In a year? In five years?

Alongside that, since unschooling is about creating an environment for learning to replace school, ask yourself tons of questions to explore your understanding of learning. You've been learning for many years, so how's that been working for you? How would you define real learning? What does a test really measure? How much of what you learned in school do you still remember? What's the difference between what you remember and what you don't? Do you better remember the stuff that was useful to you? Interesting to you? Have you learned things on your own since leaving school? What about hobbies? Is that learning any less valuable just because it was done outside a classroom? Is there a difference in how easily you learned things you were told to learn and things you wanted to learn?

Spend lots of time with your children, both hanging out and enjoying their activities with them. You will learn a lot about them, and you'll begin to see unschooling in action. It's beautiful. And when you're not busy playing with your kids or pondering the nature of learning, continue reading about unschooling and its underlying principles. Even though what you're finding might seem incredibly unconventional right now, try to keep an open mind. When I first began reading about some of the parenting things unschooling families were up to I remember thinking, "Well, we won't be doing that." But instead of feeling defensive, I just let it flow by and kept reading—I was so curious! I hungrily absorbed all the unschooling information and discussions I came across. The way they described learning aligned so closely with both my personal experiences and my observations of my own children's learning, that I knew there was something to this unschooling thing. I kept observing. I kept learning. And in a few months I was doing many of those things I initially dismissed—they began to make sense to me as my understanding grew.

If possible, maybe you'd enjoy spending some time with unschooling families to see them in action. Do a bit of web searching for unschooling or even homeschooling groups in your area (there's a good chance you'll find some unschoolers in the homeschooling groups, especially groups focused on social activities).

Some things to ask yourself: What do the parent-child relationships look like? Be careful not to put higher expectations on the kids, unschooling kids aren't "perfect," nobody's perfect, but do they seem happy? Connected? Do the parents seem supportive and available? Do the parents and kids enjoy being together? Try to observe in different situations—groups and individually. Talk with them. Or just listen. You're not there to judge, but to see unschoolers in action; to see some of the unschooling principles you're reading about play out in person; to deepen your understanding.

Personally, I did not find any reasonably local unschoolers so I focused on reading, reading, reading. I'm not one to ask questions at first, I prefer to join communities and lurk for a while, reading and trying to make sense of things for myself in the beginning, eventually asking questions about what is still confusing or nagging at me— like my six week question. It helped a lot, and I don't think I asked anything else for a few months.

But that's just *my* learning process. It's not to say that

asking questions while you process things is wrong, not at all! Some people learn more effectively that way, and it brings those topics up for discussion in the group for others to read (like me!) so it's helpful that way too. It's interesting to notice different learning styles. Why? Because the ways our children prefer to learn may be significantly different from our own. That's a *really* good thing to notice. Don't presuppose anything: observe and chat and discover. Learn.

What to Do instead of School

You're feeling an incredible swirl of both excitement and trepidation: you've decided to try unschooling! You understand that you, and anyone else in your family who has been in school, will be deschooling for a while.

But without school, what will you actually *do* all day?

It's a great question! And now we have some seriously fun stuff to talk about!

A Season of Saturdays

To help get you in a relaxed and open mindset (better for *your* learning!), try thinking of your days over the next while as a season of Saturdays. If you find yourself waking up and thinking, "It's Monday, time to get back to work and learning," try to catch yourself before you put that filter firmly in place: "Oops, I forgot, it's Saturday!"

What would you do with your children if it was Saturday? Weekends are typically a time to relax and follow the flow of the day rather than an imposed schedule. Would your kids enjoy sleeping in? What a wonderful part of the transition away from imposed schedules: sleeping as much as their bodies would like. Or are they early risers? Now they can savour the beauty of early morning without the pressure of getting dressed, fed, and out the door. Or are they a mishmash of both? Now they can learn about themselves, discovering their own unique patterns for sleep, figuring out how to better support their own needs.

Are there places you and your kids have always wanted to visit (or visit more often) but you haven't had the time? Now you do! The museum? The science centre? The art gallery? Cool! But remember, you don't need to lead your children through them, making sure they see all the exhibits. (If you're tempted to do that, take a moment to think about what it really means to get your money's worth—is it quantity or quality?) Instead, follow their curiosity. Look at the map with them, chat about what they'd like to see and do, let them navigate you around—*if* they want to. If they are engaged and excited at a particular exhibit, let them stay as long as they want. (Hint: the best learning is happening there!) If you only hit three exhibits that day, no problem, it's not a competition. If you breeze through them all in a couple of hours, that's fine too! You hit breadth instead of depth. Both are perfectly appropriate: you are following their interests, seeing their minds in action. For me, the fun was in seeing over time how each visit was uniquely its own. And as I got to know my kids better, I started seeing connections between how a visit played out and the other things that were happening in their lives. It's all connected. It's all learning.

How about something a bit closer to home? What about playgrounds? Maybe explore a different park in your town each week. Hiking trails? You can go every week or two and see how things change as spring arrives, or fall. Or rainy season. Find the things that catch your children's attention and follow up over time. Would they like to try bowling? Or laser tag? Or trampoline? The bonus is that family places are much less busy during the week—most of the kids are in school! We even scheduled our vacations in the off-season: lower cost *and* less crowded.

If you live in the city, take trips beyond the suburbs and explore farms and parks. Take a horse-drawn carriage ride. Visit a pumpkin patch in October. If you live rurally, take trips into the city and explore the attractions. Walk the streets and admire the tall buildings. Take a subway ride. Explore the world around you, not just the one outside your door.

Tired yet? Haha! I have given you a pretty wide range of ideas to help kick-start some conversations with your kids, and I'm sure you will come up with many more. That's another great thing to do with your kids now that they're home: talk. It's pretty unlikely that they are going to be interested in all of these things—certainly not all at once. But don't be stressed if your children aren't interested in even a handful of them. We're all uniquely ourselves—find out what *your* kids are interested in.

Meet Your Kids

That leads nicely into this really important piece of the deschooling journey: getting to know your children. Understanding them is the foundation from which you will explore the world together. What are they doing when you see their faces light up? What do they ask to do regularly? What new things would they would like to try? What brings them joy? What engages them so completely that they don't notice time passing? Do those things often.

Bring in related things you think they might also enjoy. If they like SpongeBob, would they like to do a puzzle depicting a scene from the show? Or if they like a certain movie, might they enjoy watching the gag reel or the short documentary about the movie on the DVD? You don't necessarily need to ask them, just let them know it exists and see if they are drawn to it. Or do the puzzle or watch the extras yourself—maybe they'll join you. Be careful though, that these are things you think they will enjoy, not things you *wish* they would enjoy. (Like that SpongeBob math workbook you were eyeing at the supermarket—skip it and keep deschooling!) And if they aren't drawn to something you give to or show them, don't fret—you've just learned something new about them. Maybe your guess was off a bit for now, or maybe they were busy and it will catch their attention next week, or next month, or next year. Their world is still a bit bigger because now they know that such a thing exists.

And don't forget about home. Life can be fun and interesting there too! What do your children enjoy doing in their PJs? Board games? Card games? Twister? Red light, green light? Colouring books? Crafts? Puzzles? Building forts with couch cushions and blankets? Carving snow sculptures after a big storm? Playing catch? Hula hooping? Making their own playdough? Kicking a ball around outside? Frisbee? Reading stories together? Playing hide and seek? A tent in the backyard? Watching movies? YouTube videos? Somersaults and handstands? Running in the rain? Jumping in the puddles? Playing video games? Online games? Baking cookies? Acting out TV shows? How could I forget Lego and K'Nex and Duplo? The possibilities are vast.

Whatever they enjoy, do those things with them. Bring bits of the world to them that you think they'd find interesting.

Remember, it's Saturday! Relax and enjoy your time together.

How Do You Learn?

I remember when my daughter was younger and her friends would comment to her about how boring her life must be without school. What do *you* think? Does it sound like life without school will inevitably be boring? I don't think so!

As you dive into all this fun living with your family, don't forget to take some time yourself to continue learning about unschooling. The challenge at this point is probably that you're feeling overwhelmed. There is so much information coming from so many places:

- observing and engaging with your kids;
- contemplating memories dredged up from your school career;
- reading more and more about unschooling and the parenting that supports that lifestyle;
- hanging out with like-minded people to see how they approach things;
- philosophically pondering about how you want to live your life; and
- questioning, well, everything!

How are you going to connect it altogether to paint a cohesive picture of unschooling?

Well, how do *you* like to learn?

Do you learn things more effectively through writing? Do you like to journal? You can pick out a beautiful notebook (or decorate one yourself if you feel so inclined) and fill it with observations and thoughts and ideas as your family moves through deschooling. Or maybe you'd like to create a blog, either a private one for your family's eyes only or a public one where you share the ups and downs of your journey with others.

Or do you like to process information more visually? Like taking pictures? You can create photo essays, grouping them through the threads you see in the images. Or maybe a photo blog if you would like to share with others.

Or do you lean toward verbal processing, enjoying conversations with others on the same journey? You can find local unschoolers and meet up to chat at park days or coffee nights, you can attend an unschooling conference or gathering, or you might approach some unschoolers you've met online and see if they are interested in chatting by phone or Skype.

Maybe it's an eclectic mix of all of these, but figuring out how you like to process information and bring together the connections of learning is a worthwhile step in deschooling. It helps you discover the vast array of ways that people learn outside school, opening you up to all the ways you might support your children's exploration and learning. And that's where the real fun of unschooling is.

Don't Rush

The key right now is building strong relationships with your children—really getting to know them. And being open and allowing them to better understand you as well. Try to consistently move forward towards unschooling, while being careful not to make so many changes in quick succession than your family loses its footing—you don't want to pull the rug out from underneath them. Sandra Dodd has a great saying for new unschoolers: "Read a little, try a little, wait a while, watch."

If you've just pulled your kids from school, or decided to stop pushing your school-at-home schedule, it's likely that your priority right now will be exploring how they will learn things without being told what and how to learn them. For unschooling to work well in your family, you need to understand and become comfortable with how people learn outside school.

Here's a tip: during this season of Saturdays, beyond not pulling out workbooks or sitting them in front of an online video lesson, be careful not to take a natural moment and turn it into a "lesson."

Why?

Because it interrupts *their* brain, the way they are thinking and connecting pieces together in that moment, and makes it about the way *your* brain is processing what's happening. What they are getting out of a moment may be very different from what you are getting out of it. And that's okay. Perfectly okay. So instead of jumping in and taking over, focus on your children. Try to notice the clues they are giving you. Often by observing what their *next* action or comment is, you can discover what *they* are taking in and focusing on. Figure out what they are seeing and learning. This is what I mean when I say "see things through their eyes"—which I say pretty often. By doing this over and over and over, you will begin to see how people learn without coercion and outside direction. Observe your children carefully. Not only will you begin to see unschooling in action, you will also get to know your children better. Lovely!

And remember, this process takes as long as it takes. Stop as soon as you catch yourself trying to direct their activities, or trying to entice them into an hour a day of reading or into writing in a journal. The key word here is *entice.* If you offer to read to them and they happily join you, great! If you think they really might enjoy a journal of their own to write or draw in, take them out to choose one, or surprise them by bringing one home the next time you go out. Part of deschooling is about discovering *your* motivations and expectations and then being careful not to put them on your children; help them discover their own. It's not the end of the world if you catch yourself slipping into the role of teacher—just stop, regroup, and start again. Observe instead of direct. I did warn you that you'll have most of the deschooling to do, yes? But I promise that there is so much fun in the observation! Children are amazing learners when they are immersed in their interests and passions. And so are we.

Embrace Passions

One thing that can often trip up a parent during this season is how passionately a child can dive into an interest that has been restricted up to this point. Often I see parents worry about "too much" TV or video games. The key here is that whatever the activity, it has been restricted. Once it is no longer restricted, there's a good chance they will take advantage and indulge to their heart's content; and that may take some catching up! Another issue is that they may worry that this reprieve is only temporary and try to fill as many hours with it as possible in anticipation of losing that freedom when you eventually (in their minds, inevitably) change your mind. Especially if you've been back and forth about it before. It will take time to build trust with them that this freedom won't be revoked. As they begin to trust that they are free to choose to play or watch any time, and they fill up on what they felt they were missing while the activity was restricted, they will begin to feel safe and free to make other choices.

If you find yourself in this situation, maybe ask yourself some questions surrounding the issue. Would I be worried if their passion was reading? Or sports? Is it the time spent that concerns me the most? Might this be their life's passion and they're happily putting in their 10,000 hours? Might readers become writers? Gamers become programmers? Movie watchers become directors? Do I only feel comfortable if I think of this time as training for a career?

What did you put many hours into as a child? Did it become your career? If not, was that time wasted? (I put thirteen years into ballet and dance yet I didn't become a professional dancer in the end. Time wasted? No way. It was my window to learning about myself.) Are your children engaged and happy and challenged? Do they work hard to figure things out and progress? Even through frustration? Isn't that pretty cool?

There's also the possibility that this is their learning tool of choice for now and you won't see their passion wane over time, maybe for a long time. But the great thing is, alongside their playing or watching, you'll be spending lots of time *with* them, observing them, chatting with them, helping them explore their interest. So if it doesn't begin to fade with time, it's very likely that in that time you'll get to a point where you're comfortable with it as a learning tool. *Anything* can be a window to the world. And to learning about themselves.

Explore Routines

As you examine your motivations, your expectations, your understanding of learning and living, it's conceivable that you will start to question the myriad of rules that surround us every day. This can be a great source of questions to ponder yet, if the process gets tiring, it can be tempting to throw your hands up in defeat and declare your family rules null and void. Try to avoid that. Don't destroy the foundation their lives have been built on. Instead, replace it slowly, brick by brick.

Hard and fast rules *are* better examined—at least once somebody balks. Dinner at 6 p.m.? Bedtime at 9 p.m.? Why? What purpose does it serve? Is there another way to accomplish that purpose? Talk about the rules, share your thoughts, listen intently and respectfully to them (in relaxed moments, not when the energy of power struggles is in the air).

One thing that might help is to shift your perspective from rules to routines. Let's peek at bedtime. People get tired. Is the goal getting to sleep when tired? Might circumstances change day-to-day? Do they for you? Are you sometimes really tired at 8pm? Other nights not until 10 p.m.? Midnight? What would be different if you thought of bedtime as more of a routine to help your children get to sleep when they are tired, rather than a fixed rule regarding the time on the clock? Does it seem reasonable to you to help them listen to their bodies and follow its cues, rather than try to control their bodies based on outside factors? No matter your answers, it's better to know what you think and to act from that place, rather than to blindly follow rules.

Another helpful aspect of thinking in terms of routines rather than rules is that for many kids (and adults!) there's comfort in routines, in knowing what to expect. Routines help with transitions: a relaxing routine to get ready to go to bed when they're tired; a routine to get ready to go out the door so things aren't forgotten; a calming routine to move through frustration, etc. It's all about getting to know and understand your children. And yourself.

Be patient. Deschooling is a time of stretching and growing and analyzing and playing and learning and observing and exploring and being together with your family. It's challenging and it's beautiful. It's work and it's play. Remember to enjoy the moments.

Do Classes Hinder Deschooling?

In my family, deschooling officially began during March Break of 2002. In Canada, March Break basically means the kids have a week off school. Many families in our neck of the woods trek down to Florida to enjoy warmer weather and long lines at the amusement parks. Instead, we were enjoying being home together. I had been researching homeschooling for a few weeks, having recently discovered it, and had been talking about it with my husband. During that fun and relaxed week, having found no discernible downside, we realized that we could just give it a shot and see how it went. We could find no compelling reason to wait until the end of the school year—three months seemed so close and so very far away at the same time. When Friday night came we asked the kids if they'd prefer to not return to school on Monday, and all three jumped at the chance. So they just didn't go back. I made the required phone calls to inform their schools, sent my letter to the school board, and we continued on at home as if our March Break vacation just didn't end.

My kids were not remotely interested in anything that looked like school so there were no extracurricular activities, no community recreational classes. They had so much lost time with their interests to make up for! And when they were interested in something, their preference was to dig into it themselves.

Swimming classes? No thanks.

Workshops at the local science centre? Nope.

Summer library program? Nah.

Hmm. I was a bit flummoxed. What should I do now? The answer was (which I know now because hindsight is 20/20 and all that): deschool some more. Sure, those activities may be fun for many kids, but my kids were happily busy with their own stuff.

On the bright side? I didn't push, I just offered and observed. And eventually I came to realize what I was doing: reaching for learning situations that, although they weren't school, looked a lot *like* school, because that was all I really knew. D'oh!

Unsurprisingly, my kids deschooled much faster than I did, so it was really helpful to my process to watch them in action. I joined them in their activities, played games with them, read to them, watched TV and movies with them, went to local parks with them; in short, had fun with them. That was how I began to see that there were so many ways to learn things beyond the teacher-student paradigm. It was, and is, beautiful!

If they had taken me up on my offers of classes, or if I had insisted, we all would have taken much longer to discover the learning that surrounds us every day and our natural ability to pursue it. Classes would have continued to be valued as a way of learning above other options. In other words, deschooling would have taken even longer.

I think that's a crucial, and challenging, step in the deschooling process. Classes are so highly valued in our society that it can be an easy way for us, especially at first, to justify the success of our homeschooling adventure to others, as well as to ourselves. "Oh, Johnny is going to weekly swimming classes, just finished a robot-building workshop at the science centre, is going to the overnight program at the zoo next week, and is signed up for hockey this winter!" That rollicking list might calm down Aunt Sally for the time being, but really, it clutters your vision and makes the real learning that happens through every-day living harder to see.

How might you figure out if your child's slate of activities is hurting deschooling more than it is helping? What really matters is the motivation behind them. Are we as parents encouraging Johnny because we feel these activities are a "better" use of his time than playing around at home? Is Johnny really excited to be there? Or do you get the impression he's going to assuage his own fears that maybe he's not learning much on his own?

Motivations that stem from external judgments rather than internal interest are clues that some more deschooling is in order. Maybe Johnny's having fun each week, yet you begin to realize that you're latching onto it and giving it power beyond "he's having fun." That's a sign for you to take the time to work through why that is, without spoiling his fun. If Johnny's not enjoying his time, remind him that he doesn't have to go and take a moment from time to time to unobtrusively point out the learning he's doing outside the class.

The big question is, are you, like me in the beginning, offering up classes or lessons as your first response when your child says they are interested in something? That's a major clue. Stop doing that. For now, challenge yourself to think of other ways to meet and expand their interests; and there *are* other ways, you might just have to work harder to find them right now. Deschooling. It's worth it. It helps you see the bigger picture; it helps you discover the world of learning that is waiting outside the classroom.

Do they like the water? Take them public swimming regularly. Visit a nearby lake to play in the water. Rent a paddleboat. Float with life jackets. Blow bubbles in the water. Take a snorkel and mask in the bathtub. Set up the sprinkler to run through or a small wading pool. In short, help them enjoy the water. Over time, you'll see them learning. From blowing bubbles, to putting their face in, to dunking their heads, to jumping off the side of the pool or dock—it's beautiful to watch, and not a swimming lesson in sight. Maybe there will be eventually; maybe they'll want to learn more formal swim strokes or water rescue techniques. But the point is, you'll discover that there doesn't have to be.

Eventually both you and your children will realize that classes and lessons and textbooks are just a few of the options on the huge learning platter of life and they will have no intrinsic value over and above any other offering. Their choices will be based on what they're interested in and how they personally like to learn things. Not on anyone else's expectations about their learning. And neither will yours! Because we're all learning, all the time.

Another step on the deschooling journey.

Shifting Philosophically to Unschooling

"My daughter has dumped all of our blocks on the floor, determined to build a tower to the ceiling. Meanwhile, her younger brother has excitedly grabbed his construction helmet and declared that any building over four stories needs to be demolished, and her older sister is complaining bitterly about all the noise because she's trying to watch a documentary. It's a messy scramble like this every day. Right now I don't need to know the rationale behind unschooling, just tell me what to do to get them to stop arguing!"

Does that scenario sound familiar? Have you brought a similar question to experienced unschoolers and been frustrated by the vague nature or spectacular range of the responses?

Sorry!

But it's because there *is* no one "right" answer. Each person in that scenario is a unique individual with a distinct personality, particular interests and goals, and their own knowledge base. We can pass along some principles to guide you, share what worked in similar circumstances with our families, and maybe brainstorm some ideas to help get you started, but you're still going to need to do some digging and figure out what will work with *your* unique family. And then tweak it, over and over, as each of you grows and changes with time and experience. Relationships aren't fixed entities. Ditto for learning: your children likely have disparate interests, varying ways of pursuing them. Even what they each get out of the same experience will often be different.

Instead of learning *what* choices experienced unschooling parents make in similar circumstances and trying to mimic those, it's more effective to learn *how* they make those choices.

How did we figure out which principles were most applicable in similar circumstances? How did we choose which actions to try, evaluate how they worked, and use those clues to move forward? How did we incorporate our understanding of each of our children's personalities into our actions?

Interestingly, that's really similar to one of the paradigm shifts I discuss in *Free to Learn*, with respect to helping our children learn: "Instead of learning *what* choices to make, it's better to learn *how* to make informed choices." In that chapter I talk a lot about how giving your child the room to gain experience with making choices not only better supports their learning in general (by pursuing the connections that most appeal to them), but it also gives them lots of experience with decision making that will benefit them throughout their lifetime. That it is applicable across differing circumstances speaks to its strength as a fundamental principle about learning.

Sure, mimicry may be helpful for a little while as you gain more understanding: "fake it 'til you make it." Some people find that a constructive part of their learning process. (How do *you* prefer to learn new things?) But don't stop there. Real learning, learning that is understood and remembered, isn't about copying a successful or experienced person's actions. That's more like memorizing. The problem is that when a new situation arises, you're stuck. You have to go back and ask, "Now what?"

Real learning is understanding the principles and processes *behind* the actions and how they fit into your personal world view well enough that you can do some analysis and make your own informed choices, in any environment or situation. And specifically, as parents interested in creating a thriving unschooling environment, you want to gain experience in making choices that are compatible with unschooling.

As you more deeply understand how unschooling works, you'll find your trust in the process, and in your children, growing. You'll find your fears diminishing. You'll find your reactions to the negative opinions of others less ... fiery. You'll probably find your urge to prove others "wrong" and yourself "right" falling away: convincing others is no longer needed to boost your own confidence. You *know* what's working for your family. And why. And that's enough.

One other thing to keep an eye out for as you learn about the philosophy that underscores unschooling is your filters. These are your closely held beliefs that can alter how you interpret what you see and read, often without you even realizing it's happening—that's how deeply ingrained they can be. The way a blue gel over a stage spotlight can give the scene a nighttime ambiance, years of school experience can have you straining to see school-type learning when you watch your children in action. It can take a while to remove that filter and truly see the real learning that is happening all the time.

So if you find that each new twist in life sends you reeling back to the unschooling drawing board, remember: understanding the philosophy, the principles and concepts that underlie our everyday actions, will help you more confidently make choices that better support your unique family members.

In any situation. Forever. That's real learning.

Shifting away from Conventional Wisdom

This is an incredible moment in human history. The ability to communicate and share ideas with other like-minded people across the globe has surged into our daily lives over the last decade, challenging our beliefs more deeply and swiftly than has been possible before. So many conventional paradigms are being challenged: health, life-style, and more and more, education.

Without access to the Internet I'm not sure I would have even come across the idea of unschooling. I mean, I questioned some conventional parenting wisdom on my own—just observing my own young children and trusting my instincts led us to an attachment parenting lifestyle before I knew such a model existed. But questioning the education system as a whole? Not on my radar. My eldest was in school through grade four—with me working with his teachers year after year in an attempt to make it a more palatable experience—before I discovered that participation in the public education system was optional. It took that long because nobody in my network of friends and family had ever challenged that convention. But when you start questioning something nowadays, you can ask a vast-ly bigger virtual audience than the face-to-face community that surrounds you. You can ask the world.

Regardless of the initial inspiration—whether you commonly challenge the status quo or specific issues have arisen that are now encouraging you to ask questions—a paradigm shift is the culmination of two discrete, yet connected, actions: shifting away from something that doesn't seem to be working for you (typically a conventional viewpoint), and moving towards an idea that seems to better align with your understanding, experience, and goals.

Let's look at a couple of the conventional ideas that are often the first to fall as people philosophically find their way to unschooling.

A conventional idea about learning: Learning needs to be directed by a teacher and measured by a test.

Often one of the first conventional paradigms that is challenged as people find their way to unschooling is the idea that for learning to happen it needs to be directed by a teacher and measured by a test (and then a midterm, and then a final exam). It's a pretty ubiquitous idea, I mean the entire public school system, and much of the private, is built around this premise. So what might cause you to begin to question it?

Maybe you had a frustrating school career. Looking back, you may come to realize that you learned just fine on your own when you were pursuing your hobbies, but that the required subjects at school or the way they were presented just weren't interesting enough to keep your attention. Or maybe over the years you realized you just aren't very good at taking tests—you knew the stuff, but couldn't get it across on the test the way the teacher wanted. Did that mean you didn't know it? Even when you used that knowledge day-to-day? Did your less than stellar test scores tell the real story?

Or maybe you're drawn to evaluate the process itself. Who chooses what everyone should learn? Why? How do they make their choices? From what perspective? Who is the customer in the learning transaction? The learner? The parents? The company that may hire the student as a graduate? How does the business of education, the enormous industry surrounding the creation and selling of curricula and standardized tests, affect the product? What's the motivation behind the curriculization (damn, that should be a real word!) of all manner of things that make up being human, like character and sex?

Maybe you dig into the idea of curriculum—*is* that really how people learn? Does everyone's learning path march the same equidistant steps, to the same beat, as the curriculum developer envisions? Through your hobbies, maybe you're recognizing that your learning process thrives on following the unique path of questions and connections that arise for *you* as you delve into a topic. Is it important to normalize as many students as possible into following the curriculum's specific path? Why? If they don't fall into step, what is the long-term consequence?

Once one thing, *some* thing, tweaks a person to start questioning this conventional idea about learning, there are so many facets of the educational system that seem to be at odds with helping children learn. Not children as a concept, as a norm, but real children. Your children.

A conventional idea about parenting: Parents need to set boundaries for their children, and a definitive no helps the parents stay in control.

Another conventional paradigm that is often challenged early as people learn about unschooling is the idea that parents need to be the boss of their family and keep their children inside arbitrary lines. Training a child to do as they're told often starts early and doesn't let up: parents, teachers, coaches—any adult in a conventional supervisory capacity demands it. What might cause you to question this paradigm?

Maybe you remember moments from your childhood when you did what you were told but it didn't work out well—you're quite certain things would have been better if you had followed your instincts. You felt deeply misunderstood. Maybe your rebellion was so fierce and damaging that you are looking for ways to break that seemingly inevitable cycle with your own children.

If you're drawn to pondering the necessity of power struggles, maybe you begin to question the conventional wisdom of being firm in all your decisions so that your children aren't constantly challenging your boundaries. Meaning, wear them down until they stop asking. Maybe you wonder if there's another way to look at the situation: "Hmm. That doesn't seem safe. What are you trying to do? Maybe we can figure out a safer way to do it." In other words, is it possible to work together rather than struggle against each other?

Or maybe seeing your children's play in action causes you to question whether seemingly arbitrary boundaries interfere with their everyday joy and learning. You watch your children as they throw themselves wholeheartedly into the activity at hand. *Look at that concentration! Do I real-*

ly want to disturb it? Is my need for, say a tidy playroom before we go to bed, more important than my children's passionate engagement? Look at them trying to build that tower over and over and over. What's the worst that might happen if I let them keep at it for now? If they ask me bring them more supplies from the cupboard, should I? Is saving them for a hypothetical "next time" more important than giving them what they need to continue digging into it right now?

Again, once a parent begins to question their role, they begin to discover how much of our conventional parenting wisdom is geared to controlling our children to make our lives easier today, rather than to raising thoughtful and interesting human beings that, in turn, are a real asset to society. Not because they fit in, but because they stand out; not necessarily in any over-the-top fashion, but in their day-to-day lives, in their family, in their chosen communities.

Learning about the philosophy of unschooling is often sparked by something that challenges us to begin questioning the conventional ideas about learning, parenting, success, and the path of school-college-job. These ideas were often handed to us without question by the adults in our lives as we were growing up. Whether or not these conventional paradigms end up working well for you, it's important to question them, to roll them around in your mind, to see how they fit with *your* understanding of yourself, of the world, and of your goals. The key is realizing you have a *choice*. The philosophy you choose to live need not be foisted upon you by others, but can bubble out of you with determination, care, and joy. That's living joyfully.

Moving toward Unschooling Principles

The second part of the shift encompasses moving toward the ideas, or principles, that seem to better align with our understanding, experience, and goals. Let's continue with those same examples. The first conventional idea about learning was that it needs to be directed by a teacher and measured by a test. Let's imagine that, for some reason or another, this doesn't mesh well with your experience. What might better align with our intuition about how we learn?

An unschooling idea about learning: Learning is everywhere.

So how might we get there?

Maybe we start by asking ourselves what we mean by learning. What is real learning? Does learning need to be hard? If it's interesting and fun, is it still learning? Is it really learning if we forget it a few weeks down the road? What kind of learning do we remember in the longer term? The things that make a connection to something we already know? That expand our perspective? The information and skills we use regularly in our lives? Those related to our interests and passions?

In shifting away from the idea of learning paths dictated by others, some might ask themselves questions about what learning is important to an individual. Is there a definitive timeline for learning? What would the consequence be if we forgot some of the things we've learned? What if they haven't come up again in our lives for months or years? What if we didn't spend the time learning them before we forgot them? What if we wait until there's a need or a connection or an interest? Is there a downside to not knowing something before there is a need or an interest? Might you learn something faster when you are interested in gaining that information or skill along the way to satisfying a current need or goal?

Then maybe we wonder about where and when real learning happens. If we feel that limiting our definition of learning to the attributes of school (desk, classroom, teacher, school hours) doesn't do it justice, how does that open up our understanding? Is it still learning if it happens at 9 p.m.? In our backyard? In our pyjamas? On our bike? If it's inspired by something we see on TV? Or hear a friend talk about? Is there any reason to value one source of learning over another? One method over another? Is it enough that learning happens? Think about your own light bulb moments. What were you doing? Were you interested and engaged? Immersed in the flow of the moment? Were you inspired to rise to the challenge, instead of turning away from it?

Once you start looking for the learning instead of the teaching, it's as if a whole new world opens up. When you stop judging the method and just look clearly at your child's engagement and joy, you can see their mind hard at work through the window of their words and actions. You begin to recognize the learning they are doing all the time. Time and location and teaching become irrelevant. Exploration of the world becomes exciting. Being curious about things that catch our interest becomes a fundamental trait.

An unschooling idea about parenting: Why not yes?

The realization that exploring the world through their interests and passions inspires so much real learning often gives rise to another paradigm shift: from automatically saying no to most of your children's requests to taking a moment to seriously consider saying yes. Your growing understanding that the best learning happens when your child is interested and engaged means that when there is something they are interested in exploring, it behooves you to take a moment to see if you can find a way to say yes. You discover you *want* to find a way to support their exploration, not stop it in its tracks.

That realization inspires an avalanche of self-inquiry. Do you really need to sweep the floor first? Get dinner on the table at 6 p.m.? (You begin to question both the time *and* place of that scenario.) Is it really a big deal to leave the in-progress board game on the dining room table overnight? To let your kids sleep in their clothes? Or stay in the bath for over an hour? To watch the rest of the movie they're enjoying even if it's past 9 p.m.? It's okay to question the conventional wisdom of day-to-day living. It may well have made sense when it first became part of society's fabric, but does it still make sense today? For you? For the individuals in your family?

Even with this quick look at a couple of principles, it's plain that unschooling isn't just a new set of rules to replace commercial curricula and conventional parenting wisdom—it's a lifestyle. It is exciting and daunting and exhilarating and exhausting. And if the ideas don't make sense in your experience or align with your goals, it's fine to move away from unschooling and explore other educational paradigms. It's a choice. But if the idea of exploring the world and sharing it openly with your children excites you, unschooling just might be for you and your family.

Keep learning and see where it takes you.

Don't Get Complacent about Unschooling

We learn so much about unschooling and how it works while we're deschooling. I mean, that's the point, isn't it? Yet in my experience, that learning is never "done." As a parent, I am *always* learning: learning about myself and my children as we change and grow, contemplating how our unschooling lifestyle flows and adapts to our growing experience; learning about new topics I or my children are curious about and exploring ways I can support and expand upon them. The philosophy of unschooling is consistent—yet its implementation looks different in every family, with every child, and over time.

If you have more than one child, have you discovered that your interactions are a bit different with each? It's not that *you* change, but how you interact becomes tailored to each child, and your spouse.

Beyond the different topics of conversation based on their individual interests, in what ways might your interactions with the people in your family differ?

- Do you use different vocabularies? (What words and phrases are unique to each of your relationships? Different topics from which to draw analogies and comparisons in conversation? More or less colourful language?)
- Are some more receptive to, and appreciative of, physical contact? (Are they a hugger? Not at all? Sometimes? Do they appreciate rough and tumble play?)
- Do some respond to you initiating conversations more often than others (And conversely, with some do you wait more to respond to their prompts?)
- Do some like to be helped as soon as they hit a roadblock while others prefer to spend some time trying to figure things out themselves?

As you grow to know and understand your children more deeply, you can adapt yourself to their learning and communication styles to better connect with them individually. It's about building stronger relationships. And from stronger relationships comes deeper learning.

Why is that?

Because with a strong and supportive relationship, your child will be comfortable approaching you to talk about things—and vice versa. With a strong relationship, they won't be worried about looking "stupid" in front of you so they'll ask that basic question about something that's nagging them. More learning. They won't be worried about feeling judged so they'll share their thoughts about a situation so they can talk through it with you:

more learning. They won't be worried about being punished as a result of their actions so they'll come to you to analyze situations that went awry, or, if possible, before they go awry, without worrying about being threatened with punishment: more learning.

With unschooling you want to support your children's learning as seamlessly as possible so they stay in the flow: that's where the best learning is. How you do that is unique to each child, and may change over time. Keep learning. And don't worry about how "life isn't perfect and they should learn that so maybe I shouldn't try to help so much." Believe me, life *isn't* perfect, and no matter how hard you try you won't be able to make *everything* work out perfectly. Do your best. Show your love and support through your actions. Show, don't tell.

And there's another piece to this "don't stop exploring unschooling" puzzle. Not only do we all grow and change over time as individuals, but every year they are a year older. Is that a bit too obvious? Probably, but I know I sometimes had to remind myself that even if I'd been unschooling for ten years, I'd never been the unschooling parent of a 15-year-old before, a 16-year-old. It is a different experience with each child because each child is different. The ways I connect with each of them are different, the ways I support their learning are different, the ways I help them process and analyze situations are different. As they get older some of the situations that arise are new to us as a family. I need to pay attention, always. To stay connected, to keep learning. About them and about myself. It keeps me from getting complacent with life.

CHAPTER TWO

:: learning ::

What does learning look like in an unschooling family?

Unschooling Doesn't Look like School at All

Unschooling looks like life.

Like an endlessly unfolding summer vacation, minus the warm weather (unless you live a lot closer to the equator than I do!), but with one big difference: the kids don't spend the time decompressing, burning off steam from months of strict schedules and the stress to perform. Nor are they complaining they're bored without a teacher to tell them what to do. Instead, they are busily pursuing the things that interest them.

In contrast, what does learning look like at school? The vast majority of us parents went to school, so we are very familiar with the process: there's a curriculum that dictates what we learn; a teacher that tries to help us understand it; and a test that determines if we remember it. Repeat that loop over different subjects and many years. It is an exacting process designed to meet its goal: teaching large numbers of students a defined collection of information and skills, within a set number of years.

The big question is: how does pretty picture number one accomplish the learning that so many of us have been taught to think has to look like picture number two?

To answer that, let's dig into some of the ways unschooling differs from school and why.

No Curriculum

Unschoolers don't buy into the idea that everyone needs to know a generalized (and sometimes outdated) set of skills and information by a certain age. Understanding that people are unique and will end up doing different things as adults, unschooling parents see it as more effective for their children to focus on learning the things that interest them. Those interesting things have a better chance than a generic curriculum of leading to the skills and information that will support their personal work and life as an adult. It's what they like to do now, and is likely to be a step on the path to what they will choose to do in the future. They follow their interests, their curiosity, instead of a curriculum.

What about that certain set of skills and knowledge that is needed to get along in society? Since unschooling kids are living and learning in the real world, interacting with people in their society as they grow up, they will encounter occasions where those basic skills and knowledge come in handy, and they will pick them up then.

Supportive Atmosphere

But not following a curriculum doesn't mean that unschooling parents are doing nothing. Instead, you'll be replacing it with a supportive learning environment. One based not on an outline, but on your child's interests. Instead of a teacher dispensing information and directing the children's activities, unschooling parents are actively supporting their children as they follow their interests. The children's goal isn't learning, but doing what's appealing to them. The really fascinating thing is that when living is the goal, learning is an incidental, yet wonderful and intense, process that happens along the way. *You* are the one who will see the learning, because you are the one looking for it—they are having fun and happen to be learning along the way. And in my experience, they are learning a lot!

Another way the atmosphere differs is that unschooling parents don't believe children will actively avoid learning unless forced. My experience shows just the opposite! Children are interested in exploring the world around them. Just watch a toddler who has recently learned to walk! That doesn't change as they get older, unless the adults in their lives take the enjoyment out of it by directing or forcing it.

Focus on Aspirations

Schools focus on teaching skills they believe students will need in the future. With unschooling, we pursue our interests and pick up the skills we need to accomplish our goals along the way—both kids and parents. The value isn't in the skill; it's in what you can do with it.

And the learning is much more effective as well. Remember how often a teacher told you, "You'll need to know this when you're older"? At least for me, that wasn't very compelling motivation to invest my time and energy. But what about when you have something you want to accomplish *now*? That's when the skill or piece of information has significant meaning. There is a reason to do the work to understand the information or master the skill—you want to learn it so you can continue to pursue your goal. There's also a much better chance you will remember it because it was of value and made a strong connection to your existing knowledge. That's real learning—learning that is understood and remembered.

Interact with People of All Ages

Schools group students together by age—it's the easiest way to deliver the curriculum sequentially. One downside is that the large number of students per teacher means there aren't a lot of role models nearby; students learn a lot of their social skills from their age peers, who know as little as they do.

Instead of having their pool of potential friends and acquaintances limited to kids their own age that live in close proximity, unschooling children often have friends with a wide range of ages. But without that ready pool, how do unschoolers find friends? Through their interests. Karate. Building robots. Sports. Art. Video games. A shared interest is a much better basis for a developing friendship than age.

Having friends with a range of ages also gives children opportunities to nurture those that are younger or less experienced, actively play with those with similar interests and skill levels, and learn from those with more experience. Age is just not a defining factor outside the classroom, so neither is it a concern for unschoolers growing up day-to-day in the world.

No Vacation from learning

The learning is found in the living. Once your family is enmeshed in unschooling, it's life. And there's no need to take a vacation from life. Vacations become about exploring new places and experiencing fresh surroundings; not about escaping from obligations. Every June, my youngest is still asked if he gets the summer off and we just answer, "No, we'll just keep doing what we're doing."

It's a pretty meaningless concept when life is like summer vacation.

Those are just five of the many ways that unschooling looks different than school. It's an entirely different way to live and learn!

Learning to Read without Lessons

Even if unschooling sounds interesting and makes some logical sense, it can be hard to loosen your grip on the notion that the basic skills still need to be taught: "Once my child can read and write, then I'll be comfortable letting them follow their interests."

It's true that reading and writing are useful skills to develop—they are opposite sides of the written communication coin. Yet precisely because of that, children living in the world will bump up against them frequently. They will encounter real life reasons to learn them, which is both more motivating than just a parent or teacher telling them they should, and more effective for real learning because as they learn they'll be actively using those developing skills to reach their own goals.

This kind of learning process differs from lesson-driven learning in a couple of key ways. First, there is no external timetable or schedule. And second, the definition of the skills is broader, just as the world is broader than the classroom.

Let's dig into reading.

At school, teachers need students to learn to read as early as possible because it is an efficient way for a teacher to communicate with a classroom full of students. The educational system is designed around written communication—teachers use textbooks and worksheets to share information with students and test papers to assess progress—so it's no surprise that it values early readers. It's even more challenging for young kids because they don't yet have much of a need for reading beyond school; their passion is active play. Yet children that don't learn to read on the school's timetable are sorted and labeled and judged inferior.

With unschooling, early reading is not necessary because we have the time to communicate with our children in the ways in which they are already skilled. We can talk with them, we can interpret their body language and emotions—we don't need to rely on reading. Our communication is rich.

At school, the process of learning to read is swept up in reciting the alphabet, phonics worksheets, and sounding out words. Young children are bestowed the label "reader" when they can make their way through early readers. And that's just the beginning: then they need to live up to it. They feel pressured to continue to develop at the same pace as the curriculum or risk losing their badge of honour.

With unschooling, children are surrounded by the literate environment of the real world. They come to see the real value that reading has: dialogue and directions in their video games; signs at the store to find their favourite food; stats on their game cards; websites about things they like; books and magazines filled with interesting information and stories. Yet that value isn't held over their heads as some perverse motivation to learn faster, "Sound it out yourself!" Unschooling parents happily read things for their children until they are ready to take the task over for themselves. And the learning is easier, and more effective, without that external pressure. Here's an interesting observation I've made over the years: unschooling kids are more likely to call themselves readers once they are comfortably reading *adult*-level books. That's what reading looks like in the real world.

As I mentioned earlier, the educational system is designed around written communication so being able to read is paramount to achieving success in that environment. Not being able to read puts students at a disadvantage in *every* subject. But without that constraint, unschoolers take in information just as effectively in so many other ways! You might find them watching videos (like documentaries, specialty channels, enthusiasts' videos), engaged in hands-on discovery (like science centres, museums, zoos) or playing around on their own with just about anything (like computers, video game design software, musical instruments, cameras, exploring outside). In fact, for many people, reading is not the preferred, nor the most effective, way to learn new things. With unschooling, learning is not compromised for later readers the way it is in school.

The same logic follows for fiction. Outside of the classroom there are many ways to enjoy stories beyond reading books. The world is full of stories being told through different mediums: TV shows, movies, comic books, board games, video games, plays, storytellers, audiobooks. I fondly remember many enjoyable hours reading aloud to my kids. Enjoying stories need not hinge on the ability to read.

There is a wide range of ages at which children are able to pull together the many pieces of the reading puzzle. Trying to superimpose lessons on the process implies not only that learning must be done on someone else's timetable, but that the child's interest and questions and personal connections are somehow not the "right" order in which to gather the pieces of the learning-to-read puzzle.

But don't infer that not teaching lessons means that unschooling parents are hands off. On the contrary, we are very involved in the process. It's just that instead of following a curriculum that walks students through one particular learning path to reading, we actively live life with our children. Words are everywhere. We read to them, we answer their questions about words—with direct answers, not impromptu mini-lessons. They may enjoy word-based games, or having the subtitles on while watching movies and TV, or following along in a print book while listening to an audiobook. Everyone's brain is wired differently so the things that spark connections will be different. If they aren't reading it's possible that their brains are not yet ready for it. Guilt and pressure won't make their brains make these connections any faster. Fully exploring the world through their eyes will.

I wrote an article for *Life Learning Magazine* years ago (May/June 2004 issue) about my daughter's journey to reading. I have included it the Appendix: "I Can Read, You Know!"

Outside the classroom there are so many other ways to discover and learn about the world beyond reading. And in the meantime, later readers won't feel like they're flawed—they'll pick up reading on their own timetable and just add that particular way of enjoying stories and gathering information to their already abundant repertoire.

Learning to Write

Is about Communicating

Writing is another of those basic skills that many parents are wary about not teaching when they are exploring unschooling. Just as there are real reasons to figure out reading, there are real reasons for writing. Not for gold stars, nor for marks, but to communicate. And again, school's need to develop these skills at early age is a direct result of their reliance on written communication. Most young kids prefer to actively play (and play some more). And if that is their preference, that's how they are learning the most about themselves and the world around them.

A child's need for written communication skills often doesn't surface until a few years later as their world begins to expand beyond the people that immediately surround them. Their parents no longer have all the answers to their questions. Maybe their interests expand beyond their local reach and they want to communicate with those further afield who share their passion. They want to read to gather more information; they want to write to ask questions of others or share their own perspective. Or share their stories. Or communicate socially with others. As their world expands there are so many real reasons and opportunities to write.

But before we dig into that, let's take a quick side trip and look at the physical act of handwriting. At school, having legible handwriting is important. When homework and written test papers are misinterpreted or unreadable, marks are lost. And when marks are lost, grades are lower. But when you step outside the structure of school, is handwriting nearly as important a skill? In the bigger picture, what are they trying to accomplish? Communication that persists over time. The method that produces that communication is much less relevant.

In today's world, communicating electronically has become ubiquitous. Typing has moved beyond secretaries and writers to a skill that benefits most people. The only handwriting I've done the last few years is for my own use—I'd be lost without my lists!—though even those could be managed electronically if that were my preference. Still, if a person comes across a need to communicate with another through handwriting and that communication is breaking down because of difficulty reading the messages, that'll be great motivation to figure out how to write more legibly. When there is a need, there is internal motivation and receptiveness to helpful information—there is real learning.

My eldest son learned to type well in a couple of weeks because he wanted to communicate with others in an online game. If you've read the article about my daughter's reading journey, you may have noticed that she was writing out interesting scenes from the Harry Potter books. Instead of reading assigned books and writing essays about them, unschooling kids find real reasons to write, reasons that make sense to them in the course their days and motivate them to do it reasonably well. They discover that a successful act of communication is dependent upon how well the recipient understands the written message. They discover that there are different levels of written formality depending on the situation.

And remember that they're engaged in real written conversation with another person—maybe in real time, through text or chat, maybe a bit delayed through message boards and forums, or maybe over even longer periods of time through books, magazines, and websites. Communication is not a solitary act. Learning about writing doesn't start from scratch when they first decide to give it a shot; they have been seeing it in action over the years when they read, or are read to. The reading that inspires them to respond is also a guideline for how to respond.

I mentioned my eldest son's typing skills developing through online gaming. His interest in communicating with others who were as deeply interested in role-playing video games as he was, led him to online forums and message boards. There he lurked at first—just reading and getting a feel for the tone and expectations of the community. He noticed the kinds of written communication that worked most successfully; meaning the posts that he found interesting, the ones that helped him learn more about the topic. He noticed that spelling, grammar, and punctuation made a difference in how well the poster's message came across.

When he eventually started posting, he wanted his communication to be clear so he chose to incorporate those language conventions into his writing style. There is also immediate feedback through the replies: if what he was saying was misunderstood, that's a clue; if there were no replies, that's a clue. Real communication. And you're around to answer their myriad questions, like, "Why does this guy always post stuff he knows is going to make people mad?" More learning about the interesting nuances of written communication that lie beyond the mechanics.

Or maybe they start by copying stuff they love (like my daughter and Harry Potter) and progress to adding their own ideas (she moved on to writing some fan fiction). When she was looking for feedback she posted her stories on an online fan fiction forum. Eventually she started writing stories about her own worlds. Sometimes handwritten, sometimes typed—always communicating. In her early teens her storytelling process became visual: she took up photography. Nowadays she's learning about the language and communication style of contracts and working with clients.

For my youngest at the moment, written communication is mostly about social interaction. Yet even from his texts to me I can see he is particular about grammar and punctuation. And even if not, that would be perfectly okay too. It's about the individual; it's about noticing what is interesting to *them* because that's where the useful learning is.

Life, if lived actively and open to opportunities, gives everyone the chance to learn the skills that best help them follow their unique path—written communication included. The wonderful thing is that unschooling kids have the time to explore, the time to find the things that interest them and develop those skills that will be uniquely helpful in their lives, instead of spending a significant portion of their childhood in a classroom, disconnected from life and trying to learn the skills that others think they *might* eventually need.

How can you help? Be open with your kids about your communication forays in the world. Did you write a letter to the editor of your local newspaper? Or participate in an interesting discussion in an online forum? Or receive a particularly stilted form letter in the mail that made you laugh? Share these moments with your kids. Not with any expectations of a response, but because they are interesting bits of communication in the world. Share, share, share. You are living and learning together.

Math Is more than Arithmetic

With reading and writing under our belts, let's tackle math. Because unschoolers don't slice the world into different subjects, we see a broader picture of the myriad ways math is intrinsically tangled with the world. We see math as much more than just arithmetic, the branch of math concerned with numerical computation and the main focus of school's math curriculum, certainly in the earlier years.

I was recently asked to sum up my experience with unschooling math and here's what I wrote:

"As an unschooling parent for over ten years I've seen how resolutely my kids pursue their interests and goals. Their persistence when they are curious and motivated seems inexhaustible, even through frustration and disappointment. But, as unschooling parents realize, real learning is minimal when a person is disinterested. When they need math is when they learn math. My kids encountered everyday arithmetic living and learning in the world around them: counting toys; playing board games; calculating hit points; baking food; making store purchases; measuring distance; balancing their bank account. The reasons for performing these tasks are clear, and the computational skills are picked up unobtrusively along the way—without developing the usual curriculum-induced aversion to math. And many adults living active and joyful lives have no need for more advanced skills.

Yet in the real world, mathematics is so much bigger than arithmetic and through years of exploring the world, analyzing situations, and making choices, my kids have developed solid critical thinking, reasoning, and logic skills. It's that strong foundation of mathematical thinking, along with their everyday computational skills, that I'm comfortable will continue to support them in whatever direction they choose to pursue. If at any point the interest or need to learn more advanced mathematical skills presents itself, that's when they can be picked up. The time conventional students have spent learning what they know, (say, a high school math curriculum) my kids have spent learning other things that make up their knowledge base. With a lifelong view of learning there is no value in comparing the particular ages at which people learn things. It's not a competition; there's no behind or ahead. Time is not lost, just used at their preference."

There are a few ideas in there that I'd like to expand upon.

Without Developing the Usual
Curriculum-Induced Aversion to Math

This is a big one, just google math anxiety or phobia. There are a couple of ways that school's math curriculum contribute to this phenomenon. First, with the early focus on arithmetic, math quickly boils down to right or wrong. And who wants to be wrong? Soon, many kids would rather avoid it altogether.

Second, with the focus on "show your work" for full marks, children aren't encouraged to think and play with numbers. Class time is focused on preparing kids to do well on the next test so there isn't time to explore other ways to get the answer, or why some approaches that seem logical at first can lead you astray, or to try to understand a student's intuition when there's a right answer and little written work to back it up. They are expected to memorize a process to get to the answer and repeat it *ad nauseum.* And on that test, you had better use that same method the teacher taught to get to your answer. This is often because grade school teachers aren't themselves fluent in math so they only understand the one typical method used to solve a math question. And that's not meant as a slight on the teachers—that's the way the system is designed.

I still remember, more than once, sitting around the kitchen table choking back tears because my well-intentioned dad was showing me how to work through some math problem using a different method. I knew that wouldn't be acceptable. I kept saying, "But that's not how the teacher wants us to do it!" And I wasn't math phobic at all. I ended up taking math all through university for my engineering physics degree. But the environment created through school was such that I just wanted to learn the method they wanted me to use and get on with it.

Many Adults Living Active and Joyful Lives Have no Need for More Advanced Skills

So, having taken countless math courses over my school career, was it worth it? I liked math and I enjoyed wrestling numbers for that right answer—for me it was like a game, a puzzle. And I imagine some of those advanced math skills would be useful for many practicing engineers, though in my own ten-year career I didn't use them. And I certainly couldn't use them now, though I'm pretty sure I could relearn them, if I had a need or interest.

But They Need to Know about Calculus

Just because unschooling kids don't follow a math curriculum doesn't mean they will never know that advanced mathematical topics and skills exist. Not teaching something is a far cry from actively shutting kids away from it. If they have an interest or passion in something that extends into more complex math (say, for example, computer programming or complex origami or game theory or astronomy), they may become interested in learning more. If they love playing with numbers, they may encounter it that way, as they explore deeper and deeper. The need for some people to understand and use higher mathematics exists in the world for real reasons. And it's through those reasons that interested unschooling kids will find it.

Yet there aren't a lot of careers that require advanced math skills. Many adults have no practical need for them—

myself included. One of the advantages to unschooling is that the children don't spend time learning stuff they might need to know some day; they spend time learning what they need or want to know *now*. With the corollary being when they need or want to know something, they learn it.

Strong Foundation of Mathematical Thinking

I was surfing around the web while writing this, brushing up on the reasons being bandied about for why students should learn advanced math. This quote is representative of what I found: "Many jobs and hobbies will require a quick mind that is logical and able to creatively solve problems. Each of those skills can be perfected by studying math. It may not seem like you will use the things you learn, but they will improve your mind and your ability to be flexible with what you want to do in life." (This one happens to be taken from http:// www.freemathhelp.com/math-real-world.html)

I understand the reasoning. Solving higher math problems often demands logical thinking and analysis to parse out the applicable method. But there are other paths to developing those skills beyond a math curriculum. Instead, unschooling kids gain logical thinking and reasoning skills through their experiences with analyzing situations and making choices on a day-to-day basis. Unschooling parents work hard to give their children the time, space, and support to gain lots of experience with those critical thinking skills that enable them to evaluate, compare, analyze, critique, and synthesize information, regardless of topic. Unschooling encourages that in spades. As the quote above suggests, and I agree, it's not really about the math.

Time Is Not Lost, Just Used at Their Preference

Along those lines, while kids in school are learning that math curriculum, unschooling kids aren't sitting around learning nothing. There is no void created in their lives. They are living and learning things that have meaning for them. They know lots of things useful to their lives that schooled kids don't. The point is, it's not a competition. Time is not lost, just used at their preference. If learning more formal computational arithmetic and advanced math becomes a need or interest, they can pursue it then, regardless of their age.

So here's what math looks like from my unschooling perspective. Arithmetic is useful because it's basic stuff that we use in our day-to-day lives—unschooling kids learn these computational skills by encountering the need for them as they live in the world. Critical thinking skills are beneficial to contributing to society and achieving our personal goals—unschooling kids gain these skills through gathering, analyzing, and critiquing information, making choices, and feeding the resulting experiences back into that loop as they follow their interests and passions.

And in my experience, that's a great foundation for living an active and joyful life.

What Does Lifelong Learning Look Like?

The conventional push to graduate from high school is incredibly strong. "We have a plan for you!" The implication is that mastering this specific set of knowledge and skills will allow graduates to eke out a competent adult life in society. Yet marching in unison is the message that if you want to excel in life, you need to acquire the next tier of knowledge and skills: college or university. And then grad school. Where you choose to step off the tread-mill and declare your learning "done" defines your likelihood of conventional success.

Yet with the cumulative knowledge of humanity growing at an exponential rate you'd be hard-pressed to find anyone to argue the point against lifelong learning— we all realize technology will be quite different even just ten years down the road. But to conventional society, stuck in the classroom learning paradigm of teachers and students, lifelong learning looks like more of the same: continuing education classes for adults, or maybe a stint at college as a mature student. (Funny how that age differentiator is important, isn't it? You're not just a regular student, you're a mature one.)

But which seems a more helpful way to support our teens as they move into adulthood: knowing a fixed set of information and skills targeted to the world as it sits today or knowing how to learn new things in the future?

Schools *think* they are teaching their students how to learn, but really they are showcasing only one of many ways to learn. And with their unerring focus over the many years of compulsory education the message is clear: in a classroom with a teacher is the best and only "real" way to learn. That style of learning certainly works well for some, but the majority of students are left feeling rather defeated and unintelligent. That's a big hill to overcome in adulthood before they get to feeling comfortable and competent in their own skin.

Unschooling Breathes Life into the Concept of Lifelong Learning

The idea of lifelong learning is that learning needn't stop after graduation, but it's also about content too. For unschoolers, the concept of lifelong learning expands beyond conventional society's definition of continuing to learn things as an adult so you don't become out-of-date, to mean *you have your whole life to learn things*. Knowledge and skills can be learned *at any point* in a person's life. With that paradigm shift, the importance of curriculum, of learning certain things at certain ages, just melts away. Without the artificial time line of curriculum, learning happens when it best works for the individual—not when it best works for the teacher.

So what does that look like, not being bound by a curriculum? An unschooling teen may not be able to dictate the rules of algebra on command, but their years of experience with analytical thinking puts them in great stead beside everyone else who doesn't happen to be a math major. They may not have read fluently until they were twelve, but you can't see any evidence of that now—in fact, in those intervening years they figured out so many other ways to learn and explore the world. Their creativity hasn't taken a beating at the hands of "do it this way for full marks." They continue to learn about and embrace the unique person they are. As teens and young adults, many unschoolers are incredibly interesting people to be around!

It's also interesting to consider that curricula, that fixed set of information that society assumes will launch teens successfully into the adult world, has been created with a typical person in mind. Living interesting lives and learning all they bump into in pursuit of their goals creates, in essence, a wonderfully personalized curriculum for unschoolers.

Why does it matter whose idea it is to learn something? Because when someone else is trying to get you to learn something, learning is hard. Your mind gropes for a connection to help this random piece of information make sense in your world. If it doesn't click into place, you try to stuff it into your brain—floating random bits of information that you hope will stay accessible until the test. That is much harder than when you are truly interested in something. In that case, your mind is engaged, your existing knowledge bubbles to the surface, and your brain is excited to connect each new piece of information you encounter to build a bigger picture of understanding.

Unschoolers also value understanding how they learn, not just what they learn. That doesn't mean tossing the classroom and teacher method, it means placing it as one of the many options on the learning platter, no better or worse than any other options, *except to the individual learner.* When they want to learn something they aren't at the mercy of others—they know they like to learn things and they get started. They aren't waiting for the permission. They seek out others around the world who already have knowledge and experience with the topic, You'll find them reading blogs, joining forums, meeting up with others locally: expanding their knowledge and understanding. They are in charge of their learning.

I think one of the hardest things to grasp for those new to the idea of unschooling is that when we are in control of our lives, we *want* to learn. Learning is not something that we need to be forced to do. Learning is not hard and to be avoided whenever possible. Learning is *fun* and an integral part of living, part of life. Learning *is* "lifelong" learning. We don't need the modifier, it's implicit.

CHAPTER THREE

:: days ::

What might unschooling days look like and why?

"What Will I Do Today?"

What drives our children's unschooling days?

One of the refreshing traits of unschooling children is their enthusiasm for life. From the youngest age, all children are driven to explore the world around them and learn how it works. Parents marvel at their single-minded determination: their obvious joy when they finally figure out how to communicate that they want something; the countless times they'll try to pick up that Cheerio; the tenacity with which they practice standing up and taking those first couple of steps.

And that insatiable curiosity does not fade with age unless the adults in the child's life work pretty hard to temper it. But that they often do—apparently there's a UCLA study that found the average toddler hears the word "no" over 400 times a *day*.

Why do many parents want to discourage their child's exploration? Well, exploration can be dangerous (they don't want to spend their time standing by the stairs spotting their toddler, or catching them at the bottom of the slide over and over and over, or watching closely to make sure they don't find the chemicals stored on the bottom shelf of the closet). Supervising their exploration can be time-consuming (even one typically adorned room can keep them busy for hours—needing supervision all the while) and sometimes boring (what's in the cupboard, what's behind the curtain, what does this toy taste like— the parent already knows the answer so they'd rather just tell the kid than wait for them). An emphatic "no" will suffice in all those cases.

Once a child reaches school age and enters the educational system, teachers attempt to channel that curiosity down the curriculum path. Good teachers try valiantly to catch their student's attention and spark learning by relating it to their real lives, but the fundamental separation of learning and life is a significant disadvantage that the educational system cannot overcome while children are isolated in buildings filled with classrooms.

The curriculum path also restricts teachers' freedom to dive more deeply into topics their students are actually curious about: "You'll cover that next year." Or to stray very far beyond the course outline: "You can look that up at home." Yet a students' definition of learning quickly becomes inextricably linked with school hours: "You have to go to school to learn." With this narrow and rigid definition of learning hammered home, many students come to loathe learning outside of school. Their curiosity has become a faded echo of their toddler years.

But What If a Child's Curiosity
Isn't Constantly Stifled?

Humans are driven to explore their environment and if adults aren't constantly trying to dampen or redirect their enthusiasm, that curiosity can drive their learning over a lifetime. In an unschooling family, it's that curiosity that drives learning instead of a curriculum. But what does life with inquisitive children look like?

It often looks busy, even on days when you don't leave the house, or even the family room!

It can look like large cardboard boxes lined up, enough for everyone, with the child up front wearing a train conductor's cap as they travel from imaginary place to imaginary place, you lifting the littlest one in and out, in and out. A tower of blocks stands in the corner as a destination, a pile of stuffed animals tag along as traveling companions, and the couch is an island to keep us dry each time it floods.

It can look like a huge Lego town, days or weeks spent building a contemporary community with stores and parks and homes and citizens, or a futuristic base with a control room and sleeping quarters and spaceships and aliens, or a medieval castle with an armory and a mill and dragons and townsfolk.

It can look like one child concentrating hard on playing a video game, while you read the guide for tips and tricks in between playing a board game with the others, everyone taking a moment to cheer when a boss is beat, or someone rolls a six or lands at the bottom of the longest ladder.

It can look like a puppet show put on from behind the couch, full of dialogue and sound effects and giggles, with you recording it to watch immediately after; and as you end up watching the other videos on the memory card an impromptu dance party breaks out.

It can look like a weekday afternoon at the park, winding the tire swing up countless times, with its passengers laughing maniacally as you release it, eventually their boundless energy spurring them to explore the play structure and escape down the tunnel slide.

It can look like each child in their room, one reading and writing on an online forum, one setting up props for a photo shoot, and one playing a computer game. Each wandering out once in a while to chat and grab a snack, you calling down the hallway to ask if anyone would like a cup of the tea you're brewing.

In each of those little vignettes, can you envision what is happening beneath the surface? The learning is rampant. Because the child is following their own curiosity, they dive into their interests as deeply as they want—maybe the Lego town lasts a day, or a week, or a month;

maybe they take 100 photos, or they play with perspective and take 200 more, or they rearrange the set and take another 300. Because their time is their own, they let their questions roam as far and wide as their inquisitiveness takes them—maybe the train becomes a bus, then becomes a plane, then becomes an ocean liner; maybe the forum thread leads to a video, which leads to a website, which leads to a new forum: another piece of the world to explore filled with people as keen to discuss their passions as they are.

The days themselves can look very different but the curiosity driving them is the same. What do they love? What questions do they ask? What would they like to try? Who do they want to become?

Unschooling is about helping them find answers to the questions that drive them and helping them discover both the person they are and the one they strive to be. Like *I* have questions that drive me, experiences to process, and a vision of the person I want to be. Living and learning each and every day, no matter our age.

Unschooling Days: Inside the Nest

Playing video games and watching TV.

Did you just tense up a bit?

These activities are often part of the typical days of an unschooling family. Yet they are so maligned by conventional society that I want to talk about them specifically.

Ask a friend or acquaintance why they don't like TV and you'll probably hear answers along the lines of too much violence, obesity fears, or their kids and/or their spouse just seems to zone out, like they're doing nothing at all. "They should be more active, more alive!" And interestingly, it often looks true in their lives. Their kids, their spouse, and maybe themselves, plop down on the couch and take on that zombie look, decompressing after a long day or week.

But what if you don't live a life of conventional work and school that you feel the overwhelming need to escape or recover from?

That's right up our alley! So let's explore what these activities might look like in an unschooling family. There is *so* much fun and learning and connecting and life swirling through them. And it often looks very different than it does in the more conventional lives typically being studied.

Let's Look at TV First

The enjoyment of learning about topics you find interesting through beautiful documentaries and information-packed shows is pretty easy to imagine, yes? Maybe you and your child love the ocean and are captivated by underwater life, but the idea of getting scuba certified and transporting yourselves to the Great Barrier Reef is incredibly daunting. Watching a documentary produced by people also passionate about life on the reef overcomes that quite nicely—certainly in the short term.

Alongside the value of gathering knowledge is the value of sharing stories. Over the years, TV shows have inspired countless discussions in our lives, ranging from how to treat friends and being true to yourself to ethics and religion and sex; from storytelling clichés to how to create a suspenseful atmosphere. We've let out shouts of shock, jumped for joy, paused the show for conversations that couldn't wait, waited for conversations until the show was over so we didn't break the mood, and dashed to the computer to research facts more deeply (or lately have a tablet within reach). To me, *that's* one of the major differences between typical viewers and unschooling viewers: active participation. We take it in, we roll it around in our minds, we weigh it against what we already know, and we make choices about what connects and what we let drift away. We fully experience it. We *enjoy* it.

And yes, sometimes we watch reruns of our favourite shows and/or movies to decompress and re-energize. It's a fun tool for that too! Maybe you've had a busy day or a week where you've been more out than in and you want to relax and rejuvenate. Maybe it's the tool of choice for your introverted child to recover after a group activity—even if they thoroughly enjoyed it, they need some downtime to recoup their energy. In those times, take a moment to mention that connection between activity and recovery so they notice it too. They're learning. Understanding themselves and their personal needs will help them be mindful about scheduling in downtime so they are less likely to become so overwhelmed that it affects them negatively.

With unschooling, the important thing (to support both their learning and your relationship) is having the choice.

If you've told them flat out, "No, you're not allowed to watch that show," you've probably just made them *very* curious! "Why not?" they wonder. And curiosity is an incredibly strong motivator. So now they have to either suppress their budding curiosity, or sneak around you to satisfy it. And if they do manage to find some time when you are otherwise occupied, or they are visiting friends with access (which will happen more and more as they get older), they'll be watching it without being able to chat with you about what they discover. And that means less learning. They'll also be more likely to continue watching even if at some point their inclination is to stop. Their curiosity about the source of your denial, or just plain rebelliousness to flex their power against your rules pushes them beyond their own boundaries. *That's* where more harm than good can happen.

Imagine your child is watching a scary movie at a friend's house that you've banned. If she starts to get scared halfway through the movie there's a good chance she'll stick it out to prove you wrong, or to avoid admitting her fear to her friend. Then maybe she has nightmares for a couple nights. Result? You're now even more determined to make sure she doesn't watch scary movies because you believe she's just proved she can't make good movie choices on her own. But really, you took the choice out of her hands up front—all her actions from that point were mired in reactions to your denial, not her own motivations.

With choice, and having a parent willing to watch with them, to support them by reacting to their needs in the moment—maybe pausing the show to discuss what's happening, or lowering the volume during scary or emotional scenes, or warning them when they might want to cover their eyes, or changing the channel when asked—they are free to follow their curiosity until it has been sated, exploring the world *and* themselves, in a *safe* environment. Lots of learning. In addition, it's a great opportunity for you to learn more about them. What sparked their interest? How was it satisfied? Do they seem to want more?

Does all that sound like mindless zombie TV watching?

Now Let's Look at Video Game Playing

What might gaming look like in an unschooling home? With available, willing, and supportive parents, gaming with younger children can often include reading the game text for them as they play: more stories shared, more conversations initiated, more strategies batted about. Thinking out loud can be a really fun way to sort through ideas, and a great way for parents to see their child's beautiful mind at work—while they're at play!

Parents may find themselves reading game guides aloud to their child or silently to themselves to help their child figure out how to beat that boss, or find all the gold skulltulas. When my kids were younger we had a computer in the same room where they usually played so we could look things up quickly. Sometimes we printed out a section of the guide to have handy on the couch. I have *wonderful* memories of working together with Michael to reach his goal of beating Luigi's Mansion. And of watching Joseph play for hours, deeply fascinated by the artistic style of *The Legend of Zelda: The Wind Waker* and *Shadow of the Colossus*. He'll still call me to come see beautiful scenes and characters.

One thing that can be challenging is when our children become frustrated while playing. Our first reaction may be to shy away from it, insist they stop playing for a while. And sometimes a break can be a great strategy—if they're willing to try it. Helping them explore ways to work through frustration while they're figuring out new things is a great life skill. Beyond video games, there will be many situations where things are new and challenging and understanding ways they can more comfortably move through those situations is invaluable.

Another way parents can support their kids while they play is to bring food and drinks to keep their minds alert and reaction time at its peak while they're deep in their work. More learning, not only about the game strategies themselves, but again, about the physical ways to support their brains and bodies. Be with them. Be available. Anticipate their needs, not only to support them in the moment, but to help them learn what their needs are.

I remember Joseph wanting to try online gaming about ten years ago, so we ordered a keyboard for his PS2 and figured out how to get it set up. Sure, I wondered what that world would be like. Friendly? Overwhelming? I figured we'd discover that together! Soon after he got connected I remember printing out a page of emoticons for him so he could understand the lingo. He picked up typing on his own in a couple of weeks. We found a world occupied with the same range of people and personalities you find face to face, and since then we've had countless conversations about life and people and social conventions and friendships.

I remember when we first started unschooling. Joseph was almost ten years old and he dove deeply into playing video games. At first I was uncomfortable, unsure he was learning much of anything. But when I realized my only other choice was to implement time restrictions and be stuck with the resulting power struggle, I decided to dive in with him and see what all the fun was about! One of the best choices I've ever made. A couple years later I wrote about what I learned. It was published in *Life Learning Magazine* (Sept/Oct 2004 issue). You can find it in the Appendix: "Everything I Need to Know I Learned from Video Games."

Does playing video games and watching TV look a bit different to you now? Can you see all the learning that is woven into the fabric of these activities? All the loving support that is made concrete by celebrating the joy found in them? Exploring them together with my children has not only put my mind at ease, but also strengthened and solidified our relationships.

Unschooling Days: Out in the World

What does out and about in the world look like in an unschooling family?

One of the especially lovely bits of unschooling is being free to head out and explore places when they are significantly less busy—meaning, while the vast majority of kids are in school. But timing isn't the only thing that often looks different. Have you ever shared a museum visit with kids on a school trip? An unschooling family's trip to a museum doesn't look like kids spending X minutes at an exhibit and then being told to move on. Or kneeling on the floor to scribble answers on a worksheet full of only those questions that align with their curriculum. For unschooling families, going to the museum isn't called a "field trip" and it looks more like spending as much, or as little, time at each display as wanted. Questions that cross their mind are blurted out in quick succession, or maybe their face is a study in quiet contemplation as they take it all in. To each their own style.

I also notice conventional parents pushing and pulling their kids this way and that, trying earnestly to keep their kids on their adult schedule. "Don't touch that." "Come here." "We have to leave." "No, you can't have that." "Stop whining or we're going home right now." "I'm gonna count to three." You can sympathize with their frustration even while you question the usefulness of their demands.

The difference in family dynamics in unschooling and conventional families can be quite stark. That's because there are different priorities at work. Unschooling parents work *with* their children when they are out and about in the world. Let's look at three less conventional ways we work together as a family.

Briefing and Debriefing

I believe Anne Ohman first introduced me to the idea of briefing and debriefing in this context. The terms don't describe any particular process; they remind us to talk with our kids. Before going places, let them know what to expect—brief them. Like you would ask your spouse to do before accompanying them to a business dinner. Or a friend to do before meeting up with their extended social group for the first time. Be considerate.

Take a moment to think about the kind of information your children would find useful. Will there be lots of people wherever you're going or are you on your own? Will there be certain scheduled activities (like dinnertime at Grandma's) or are you following your own timetable? How negotiable are the scheduled things? If you're exploring say, a museum, are the exhibits mostly hands off or are kids invited to touch? Is it a place where running is frowned upon or encouraged? Is there a certain time you need to leave and why? And don't expect that they will remember what you told them last time you visited. Happily and matter-of-factly let them know what's up today.

The point of helping them understand what's expected and why in different situations is to help them learn the ins and outs of the world around them. It's not for parents to have rules to hold up and scold their children when they fall short. You're sharing good information with them. And while you're out, help them as best you can to figure out ways they can be comfortable within the environment.

How might you do that? How about an example. I remember trips to the library when my daughter was still looking at books while her younger brother was done and getting antsy. I recall sometimes saying "Your brother's done, are you okay looking at books on your own while I take him outside to run around? We'll check back in with you in ten minutes." If yes, that's what we did. If no, we'd try come up with another path forward. Maybe she only needed five more minutes and I'd try keeping her brother occupied with a couple more books, or chatting about the posters on the wall. Maybe she wanted longer but wanted me close by so we'd keep thinking. Maybe I'd see if her brother wanted to use a library computer for a while, or suggest checking out what we had now, taking her brother home, and then coming back later just the two of us so we could stay as long as she liked—maybe after dinner that night or on the weekend. If we did do that, I'd remember to thank her for leaving earlier than she'd wished. And I'd do my very best to make sure we went back ourselves as soon as possible: follow through on your plans helps build and maintain their trust in you. If you let things slide, next time they'll understandably be less inclined to accommodate others' needs in the moment.

Then on the drive home, or maybe sometime later that day when things have settled down, check in with them—debrief. Did they have fun? What did they enjoy? What didn't they like? Leave a quiet and comfortable space in the conversation for them to bring up things they found challenging so you can process them together. If things went awry at any point, chat about what you might do next time a similar situation arises. Which leads to my next point.

Accommodate Personalities

If you let them know what the expectations are for a particular place or event and your child finds them too much, that's not a failure on anyone's part. It is what it is *for now*. Things change over time—this moment doesn't define forever.

And remember to think outside the box. We're an inventive bunch and there are all sorts of ways to accomplish things. Let's say you love eating out but your children find restaurants challenging—maybe the noise or activity level is too much, or they can't sit still very long at the table and start running around and disturbing other patrons, or maybe they're louder than the ambient noise level. Yet giving up restaurant dining isn't your only option; there are so many ways you might accommodate them. Let's brainstorm a few:

- bring quieter activities to keep them busy—we were never big restaurant people but the odd time we went we'd bring handheld video games to pass the time, I'd keep paper and pencils in my purse to play tic-tac-toe or hangman, and our mainstay was to play twenty questions while we waited for our food to arrive (we adults would play *with* them—don't expect them to occupy themselves);
- choose family-style restaurants so they are less formal and much more accommodating to children, like handing out crayons and activity pages and having a fun kids' menu;
- during other seasons we'd choose take out so we could eat in the comfort of our own home, maybe setting out a "picnic" with paper plates, or a more formal setup with candles, to make it an event; or
- arrange for grandparents or a family friend to stay with the kids (or the kids to visit!) while we dine out.

And I'm sure you can keep going. The point is, there are so many options that we don't need to put our kids in situations beyond what they can do. Beyond what they *want* to do—just because they happened to sit quietly through your last restaurant visit doesn't mean it's fair for you to now expect them to do it again and again.

Staying Home is Okay Too

With unschooling we talk a lot about exploring the world. But if any of your kids just aren't interested in going out very often, that's okay too! That's another difference with unschooling families. Many conventional parents expect their kids to just tag along and do what they're told. Their children's chance to explore the world on their terms is when they move out. But unschooling parents want to help their kids figure out the world and how they fit into it *now*—before they start navigating it on their own. So we work with them to accommodate their wishes as much as we can. Why is that important? Because if that's what's on their mind now, that's what their brain is itching to explore and learn about. If they'd prefer to stay home to continue digging into their activities of choice, more power to them!

What if one wants to go somewhere and another doesn't? Brainstorm! Can it wait for a time when both parents are available to split up, one home and one out? Or can multiple destinations be combined into one trip to satisfy multiple wishes?

Remember, staying home is not synonymous with being sheltered—you can bring the world to your kids. It's even easier now with the Internet at your fingertips. Use your online search skills to find websites, games, and videos that you think your child might find interesting and share them. Browse library shelves yourself and bring home new books and movies. Hit clearance sales and thrift stores for treasures to share. Just remember to do so without expectations. Even if they don't dive in for any length of time, you've introduced them to another bit of the world that they can explore if and when they become interested. And maybe it's just a season. Don't be tempted to permanently define them by their current wish to stay close to home.

And last, but not least, don't forget to search for things in the world that excite you! Like that really old atlas or dictionary or Candyland game you found at the thrift store. Or that clearance sale popcorn maker. Let them see that engaging with and exploring the world isn't just for kids. Live life joyfully *together*.

"Who Am I and What Makes Me Tick?"

What activities do I like to do regularly?

What really annoys me? What makes me smile?

What food makes me feel good physically? How much food fills me up comfortably? Am I hungry when I eat?

How much sleep helps me wake up feeling refreshed? Yet if I'm excited about something, can I push through tiredness or am I mostly cranky?

Do I think and learn better when I'm alone? Or do I prefer to bounce ideas around with others?

Am I more relaxed and attentive when I'm nestled in amongst all my things? Or in a sparse environment because clutter is too distracting?

When I'm interested in something, how do I like to learn about it? Do I sit back and observe? Research? Do I dive in? Give it a shot?

Do I like baths or showers? Morning or night?

Do I like a routine to ease gently into sleep? Or do I like to keep going until I drop, content and exhausted?

The answers to these kinds of questions paint a unique picture of who I am and what makes me tick.

Many parents make these choices for their children: "Tidy up your room before you go play." "It's bedtime—go put your pyjamas on and pick a couple books." "Your T-shirt is dirty, go put on a clean one." "Finish your plate before you get down from the table." Why? I think there are a few reasons that mix and match to varying degrees:

- These are the ways that feel best for them so they want to pass their wisdom along to their children—*they* like things tidy; *they* like to read before they go to sleep; *they* like their clothes spotless;

- They want their children to fit in smoothly with their routines—life is easier, less complicated;

- They have been told there are "right" ways to live their lives and they want to help their kids develop those habits so they aren't judged negatively by others (even if the parents themselves don't feel they measure up).

It's a noble ideal: they want their children to learn the right ways to take care of themselves so they become successful adults.

But what does this have to do with unschooling? Let's find out.

To start, I'd tweak the goal with two short but very important words: " ... want their kids to learn the right ways *for them* to take care of themselves so they become successful adults."

We all have our own definitions of "successful", but what a difference those two words make. "For them." We are all different people, regardless of our age. Think about you and your spouse for a minute. You're reasonably successful adults. Do you go to bed at the same time? Get up at the same time? (I'm more of a morning person, while my husband's been more of a night owl—huh, common phrases for different sleeping patterns.) Do you both like baths? (For us, that's him more than me—if we broaden the definition of bath to include hot tub). What about living environment? (I enjoy being surrounded by things that make me smile and if it's not in a pile I can see I forget it exists, while he mostly finds clutter distracting.) In essence, we're both pretty different in how we tick: our habits, our personalities, our likes and our dislikes surrounding day-to-day living.

Those differences are part of life, and there is no one "right" way for individuals to live; other than the way that works best *for them*. Why would we think that would be any different for children?

So, say I want my children to learn how *they* tick, why are unschooling principles a good way to go about it?

As I got more and more comfortable with the unschooling learning environment, as I saw my children's real learning in action, as I saw all the learning that comes through living, my eyes opened wider and my thoughts swirled. For me, there were a couple key observations that swayed my choice.

Firstly, this personal learning rose in importance in my eyes. With the education system's myopic K–12 view gone, I began looking at the bigger picture of their lives, seeing childhood as the growth of the *whole* person into adulthood. Digging deeper, I realized how important understanding myself and how I tick has been for all aspects of life. How exceptionally useful that information is as an adult, in both my work and my relationships, and how since figuring that stuff out, my life has been much more joyful because I am no longer working against myself (i.e., trying to act like someone else's—society, parents—vision of me). So much better! I also realized that it took a lot of time to explore and discover my quirks, my needs, my goals—and to realize that they change over time. For me, this deep understanding of *themselves* became something very important to pass along to my children, alongside their more academic learning.

Secondly, I came see it's *all* learning. Over our first unschooling months, their learning became more intertwined with our living. I began to make less and less distinction between academic and personal learning—both were happening in most situations. Their personality and current needs and ways of processing were just as vital to the learning process as was the academic knowledge or skill they were pursuing. And unschooling was supporting *all* of their learning spectacularly.

If you do choose to move to an all-encompassing unschooling lifestyle, as with all unschooling learning, the key is *when they're interested*. As their parent, you have an idea how your children tick and can make a good guess at what works for them—they've been communicating that information to you since they were born. Don't overwhelm them with choices they aren't interested in making—that's just noise. But when they are interested in trying things differently, be open to letting them explore. Like a change in their going-to-sleep routine, or in their eating habits, or in how tidy their room is, or whatever bit of life they are contemplating—that's when their interest is piqued and their learning is sparked.

There's one other point I'd like to touch on. It's common for those first hearing about unschooling to wonder skeptically, how do the kids learn to get up in time for jobs, or to do what their boss tells them, or to do any other adult thing the questioner finds distasteful, so that they will grow to be independent, successful adults who can pay their bills and get jobs. That's not a surprising question—it's a big stretch at first!

But think about it for a minute. It's actually not that illogical. Unschooling kids are making their own choices *every day* and throwing their enthusiasm behind them. When they choose to start a job, their enthusiasm to follow their choice will help them get up in the morning, more than any previous years of "training" to get up will.

Unschooling has precisely helped them learn how to follow through with their choices. And given them lots of practice in making good choices and understanding the motivation behind them. They won't see their job as a burden—one they must have trained years for by getting up early and sitting bored at a desk for long hours and being forced to do things they don't want to do day in and day out. They will also make better job choices up front. Understanding themselves, they won't pursue a job that is a complete mismatch with their personality and lifestyle. And if they choose to take one that isn't a great match, they will have other reasons, like the money, or the schedule, or the experience, and *those* will motivate and reward them for going to work. Or if their job does become a burden, they will start looking around for a better match because *that's what they've always done.* When things don't work out, they don't feel stuck; they find ways to move on. They are wonderfully prepared to be independent, successful adults.

Raising Children and Developing Character

As unschooling parents, our intuition at first and our experience soon after, shows us that our children's best learning happens when it's part and parcel of pursuing interesting things in their lives. That's when it has meaning to them and they are motivated to try to figure it out.

Why? Because people are unique. A one-size-fits-all curriculum doesn't provide the tailored body of knowledge and skills useful to a particular individual. Nor does trying to fit each child into the mould of a model citizen. As we support our children's exploration of the world to find what fascinates them, we can also support them as they dig into who they are and what drives them. Help them discover the kind of person they want to be.

Across North America certainly, character education has become part of the curriculum, trying to teach traits like respect, responsibility, self-discipline, caring, trustworthiness, fairness, honesty, courage, sporting behaviour, citizenship and positive attitude. One of the issues with that is described by John Holt in *How Children Fail.*

Teachers and schools tend to mistake good behavior for good character. What they prize is docility, suggestibility, the child who will do what he is told; or even better, the child who will do what is wanted without even having to be told. They value most in children what children least value in themselves. Small wonder that their effort to build character is such a failure; they don't know it when they see it.

It's another instance of adults trying to mould children into their singular vision of the perfect person. The problem is that what adults most often value is what makes their life easiest in the moment. That isn't surprising though, is it? We parents can find ourselves doing this too. And is it weird that what just jumped into my mind was a quote from JK Rowling in *Harry Potter and the Goblet of Fire?*

Remember, if the time should come when you have to make a choice between what is right and what is easy, remember what happened to a boy who was good, and kind, and brave, because he strayed across the path of Lord Voldemort. Remember Cedric Diggory.

Thanks, Dumbledore! Okay, maybe that's a little melodramatic. But it's about character, isn't it? If you find yourself more often making the easy parenting choice, maybe ask yourself if you're giving it your best effort. And this John Holt gem bears repeating: "they don't know it when they see it." That's a good reminder for us parents as well.

Instead of trying to mould our children from the outside, unschooling parents work from the inside, helping their children discover what works best for them. We celebrate the fact that people are different, that we are each a unique combination of personality and character and interests. It's from that place of understanding that we help our children explore the world, and themselves, and find how they most comfortably fit together.

So what does it look like when we extend the unschooling learning philosophy beyond academics and into character? Character is the unique set of qualities, or traits, that make up a person. Instead of teaching these traits, we give them the space and support to learn about them through living.

There are plenty of situations that arise that involve real choices about character—no need to make them up. And as unschooling parents we are involved in their lives, helping them process these situations, helping them see the different ways they can choose to act and react, helping them figure out the kind of person they want to be.

And by living openly alongside them, we are showing them that learning and growing and moving towards being the person you want to be is a lifetime activity. It's part of being human. I am growing and stretching and challenging myself regularly, in character development as well as in knowledge acquisition.

The need for, or usefulness of, positive character traits will come up in everyday situations, just like the need for and usefulness of other skills such as reading and writing comes up in life. The key, as always, is to support our children, not try to direct them. Help them discover why certain traits are helpful; don't demand that they exhibit them.

Let's try an example. One situation that often challenges parents is joining activities; or more precisely, quitting activities. You've probably heard some version of this parenting argument, "She needs to finish what she starts. She needs to learn self-discipline and responsibility. If we don't insist she finish, she'll just give up any time something comes along that is hard or she doesn't like."

First, I find the idea of "teaching self-discipline" an oxymoron. Self-discipline can't be imposed from the outside because it's all about internal motivation. But leaving that aside, if as a parent you force your child to finish out whatever activity you feel they've committed to—for example, a series of lessons you've signed them up for—are they really learning self-discipline?

Put yourself in the child's place. What might you be thinking about, and hence learning, if you're told you have to finish that series of lessons you signed up for? The next few times you go you're probably thinking this is a waste of time, you could be doing X, Y or Z instead. Or maybe your distaste for the subject begins to grow to colossal proportions and you swear you'll never pick up a paintbrush again (or baseball bat, or swimsuit, etc.). Or maybe you vow to never sign up for anything else again! Maybe eventually all three. I imagine that self-discipline wouldn't really be on your radar at all. But you may be soured on that activity, and on exploring any activity in this fashion.

Instead of trying to teach them self-discipline, help your children find ways to develop it. At one point they had the motivation to keep pulling themselves up and trying to walk, again and again, for example. When we have a personal goal, we'll discover how much of our time and effort we're willing to invest to achieve it. That's one of the wonderful things about unschooling: our children are encouraged to find those things they are truly interested in, to pursue those audacious goals. That, more than anything else, helps them develop self-discipline.

Has your child ever gotten frustrated trying to do something yet still continued to attempt it? A cartwheel? A drawing? A video game level? They are developing the ability to motivate themselves right there. They are continuing to pursue something despite the challenges they are facing. Those experiences show them the connection between effort and reward. And their self-discipline grows as their interests expand and the distance between effort and reward gradually gets larger. You don't have to teach this stuff, life is full of it. Instead, do your best not to short-circuit it.

I still remember the late afternoon that stretched into dinner time and I chose to forgo dinner prep and stay at the pool watching my determined daughter practice diving over and over (and over) until she was comfortable she had it. Celebrate those times when their determination is just a joy to watch in action. See those moments, not a late dinner. Remember them.

Same goes for the other traits that make up an individual's unique galaxy of character. By experiencing real reasons, in their real life, to explore and develop these traits, children understand them better than through any character lessons others might try to teach them. And as a result of this exploration, and the support of their parents during it, unschooling children are often quite knowledgeable about themselves, their strengths and their weaknesses.

Watch your children in action. They are pretty incredible, aren't they? Continue to figure out ways you can support and help them as they explore themselves and the world.

Exploring Organized Activities

It's one thing to get comfortable with unschooling in your own home, but it can be a whole 'nother kettle of fish to bring that learning mindset with you out into the world.

For example, is your child interested in taking a class or joining an organized activity? Swimming lessons? Ballet? Hockey? If you're newer to unschooling, you may want to consider avoiding structured activities for now, as they can interfere with your deschooling, but if your child is interested, let's talk about some of the ways you can support their learning and enjoyment.

The first question—is your child interested in pursuing their interest through an organized activity? For example, there's a difference between being interested in hockey and wanting to play hockey. As a child I enjoyed watching hockey (live and on TV), I enjoyed playing street hockey, and one season I enjoyed keeping my own stats for my favourite NHL team—but I was never interested in playing organized hockey (and my dad coached a girl's hockey team for a few years so it was definitely on my radar). Just because your child expresses an interest in something, that doesn't necessarily mean they want to formally participate in it, so it can help to take a moment to consider the many possible ways to pursue an interest in something.

Finding a Good Match

The typical response when a child asks to join an activity, assuming the parents agree, is for a parent to find the closest location and sign them up. End of story. From there, the child is expected to do the work to fit into the environment so they can participate.

For unschooling parents, our foremost focus is on supporting our children's learning, so instead of expecting our children to adapt, *we* are willing to do the work to search out an environment that meshes well with how our children like to learn. Understanding that the atmosphere surrounding many activities is dictated by the individual adults who run them, we look for a good fit between the group's atmosphere and the child's personality and goals.

Let's take ballet as an example. Some schools are focused on their students participating in dance competitions; some on putting together a big year-end recital; some on progressing students through formal dance examinations; some on the recreational enjoyment of dance. Or how about karate? Some dojos focus on attendance and advance their students through the belts based on time invested; some focus on skill development and advance their students based on proficiency displayed; some dojos insist their students compete in certain tournaments and some avoid them altogether.. What are your child's goals?

And on top of the approach to the activity itself, there's also the teaching methods and personalities of the teachers/coaches. Do they demand obedience and cultivate a strict, hierarchical environment? Do they encourage questions and cultivate a supportive atmosphere? Are they somewhere in between? The knowledge and skills of the instructors being relatively equal, there is still a wide range of possible learning environments—some your child may fit into like a glove while others may turn them off the activity for years to come. If your goal is to help them explore their interest, your best bet is to help them find the studio/dojo/group/league that is a good match for their personality.

What has that looked like over the years for us? With my daughter, when we moved, I continued to drive her to her Girl Guide meetings in our old community because she had a great connection with the leader (an hour each way). The next year the leader changed and she wasn't as connected, so she tried out meetings with a couple groups in our new community before finding one that suited her. When my youngest wanted to try karate, I called some of the different dojos around that we could try. And I talked about it with him in those terms: this dojo seems like a good fit so let's try it out, see if you like it, and if you don't there are others we can try.

Instead of choosing a location by geography and expecting your child to conform, take the time to explore the options and try to find one that is a great fit for *your* child.

Getting Ready to Go

Participating in an activity probably means a fixed time for lessons or practice or games. This can be challenging, especially for younger children who may have a harder time transitioning to leave if they get caught up in something at home. On top of that, it can also be challenging for newer unschooling parents because they may feel like they are coercing their child to leave. What do they do if their child says they don't want to go this week?

If going to an activity is becoming a struggle, take a moment to look at how you're setting it up. If you find yourself saying something like, "It's Wednesday, your karate class is today, are you going to go this week?" take a moment to rethink that. By asking your child each week whether they want to go to class, you're basically asking them to revisit their decision each time. That's a lot of work, especially for younger children.

In my experience, it's easier to assume your child wants to go (they wanted to sign up in the first place) and do your best to help them get there. Make it as painless as possible for them. "Your karate class is today! I have your gi clean and I put your bo by the front door. We'll get changed and leave right after dinner." By bringing it up during the day you have time for conversations without the added pressure of trying to get out the door. And by making sure all the supporting things are in place so that your child can just go to the activity (clean outfits/uniforms, working and available equipment, transportation and timing, etc.), then they can focus on the activity itself. Are they enjoying it? *That* is the real question.

Choosing to Quit

When our children express an interest in an activity it can be easy for us parents to get caught up in the idea that "maybe they'll grow up to do this for a living!" We want to encourage them to continue. We're afraid that if they quit they'll "get behind" and the opportunity to develop their interest into a career will be lost. At age eight.

There are a couple of things to consider here. First, if it's not catching their interest so much that they are excitedly dedicating many hours to it on their own, then the chances of a professional career are slim. Certainly the chances of *enjoying* a professional career are slim. Second, quitting is not a forever decision. My daughter took a couple years of dance lessons when she was young, quit, and went back for a year when she was sixteen. She really enjoyed it! When you're doing things for enjoyment, there is no "behind," there is just where you are. At the dojo there are white belts of all ages. There are adult beginner ballet classes, there are adult recreational hockey leagues, and there are public swimming times where people of all ages and abilities can enjoy the water.

Or maybe we're worried that our children wanting to quit means they will always give up when things get challenging. First, challenges that aren't motivating and inspiring for *your* child are probably not the right kinds of challenges. Great to know! But also, the choices they make today don't define all the choices they will make in the future. The choices they make today are helping them *gain experience with making choices.*

Over the years they will gain lots of experience with wanting to try something, with choosing ways to try it out (organized or not), and with seeing how well those paths meet their goals. They will discover things they enjoy and things they don't, and get a better feel for the clues that help them decide when to step up their game and when to quit something.

And even after they choose to quit something (for now, at least) they're *still* learning. How does that choice feel? Do they miss the activity? How much? What do they miss about it? What are they doing with the time that quitting freed up? Are they enjoying that more than the activity? Less? So much learning!

Or maybe we're upset about the money we invested in the lessons that we may not be able to get back. Think about it this way: the more you insist your child continue in the activity after they've decided they don't like it, the stronger their resistance to the activity will likely grow.

If you've paid $100 for a series of recreational ballet lessons and they're only half finished, might you consider that last $50 as an investment in preserving their enjoyment of dance? If they don't enjoy the lesson environment, try the myriad other ways there are to enjoy and explore dance: put on some classical music and dance around the room; try a different style of music and see what happens; borrow ballet books and DVDs of dance performances from the library; help them try out what they see; buy some costumes or a tutu so they can dress up; record their performances at home so they can see themselves; go see a ballet in a fancy theatre (*The Nutcracker* is beautiful and fun for kids, and often performed around Christmas); in the spring, check your local dance schools for their student recitals (tickets are usually inexpensive). Remember, formal lessons aren't the only way to enjoy many activities.

Supporting your children's exploration of activities outside the home by doing your best to set them up for success goes a long way to helping them discover their unique interests and passions.

And that's a great path to living joyfully.

CHAPTER FOUR

:: parenting ::

Let's talk about the kind of parenting that supports unschooling.

Attachment Parenting

Flows into Unschooling

There are discussions from time to time on whether the term unschooling is applicable for children younger than school age. Granted, in some countries school entry age is getting younger and younger, not to mention the assumption that children will attend preschool. Yet if pressed, I tend to fall in the "it's unschooling when your child is compulsory school age and instead you choose to create your own learning environment for them based at home" camp, though it doesn't bother me when people use it in conversation with me because I know what they mean. That said, it can be confusing for people new to the idea unschooling—you don't need to choose your child's style of education soon after birth—so I tend to stick with the "compulsory school age" threshold, especially since nowadays there's a pretty reasonable term available that I think pretty closely describes the kind of parenting implied by unschooling for young ones: attachment parenting.

Attachment parenting, a term coined by Dr. Sears, focuses on nurturing the connection between parent and child. From his website:

"A close attachment after birth and beyond allows the natural, biological attachment-promoting behaviours of the infant and the intuitive, biological, care-giving qualities of the mother to come together. Both members of this biological pair get off to the right start at a time when the infant is most needy and the mother is most ready to nurture. Bonding is a series of steps in your lifelong growing together with your child."

This parenting style not only supports the development of a wonderful relationship with your child, it also encourages parents to discover and learn things about themselves and their children that will facilitate a reasonably smooth transition to unschooling, should they choose to take that route. Let's talk about three of those ways.

1) Developing this bond leads to a strong and connected relationship with your child and that relationship is fundamental to a nurturing unschooling environment. You play with them, you answer oodles of questions, you

show them things you think they'll enjoy, you hug them when they're sad, you help them when they're angry, you feed them when they're hungry, and you probably feel like you're constantly changing their diapers and clothes. In other words, you live life alongside them. You're responsive to their needs. Every time you help them meet their needs, you're building a more connected relationship. They are comfortable coming to you for help. You become their trusted guide to the world around them.

2) Another aspect of this lifestyle, taking signals from your child about their needs (versus requiring them to fit into your expectations and schedule) also leads smoothly into the unschooling mindset. This is a bit different than all the connecting you're doing above; it's more about getting comfortable with your child following their interests. Each time you see your child expressing and then satisfying a need, with or without your help, you see the connection between them. Through your observations over time, you realize that their needs aren't arbitrary or random: there's a real internal motivation behind them. That experience builds trust that inspires you to help them meet their needs, even when you don't yet know what the motivation is. Unschooling at its finest.

3) Yet another benefit of this style of parenting young children is that you are observing and helping them all the time. That means you see their learning in action. Whether it's learning to turn over, or crawl, or walk, or talk, or eat, or reach for the doorknob, or pick up a toy, or any of the incredible number of other things they learn in their first few years, you are awed by their determination

to do whatever they set their mind to. As John Holt wrote in *How Children Learn*, "Fish swim, birds fly; man thinks and learns."

It's another unschooling principle brought to life. People are wired to learn, and the best learning happens when they are interested and engaged in an activity.

There's another reason I would encourage parents of young children to think in terms of parenting rather than unschooling: so they don't put more pressure on themselves. Being a parent of young children is time-consuming and often physically exhausting—I remember when I had three children ages five and under. You are their capable emissary to the world, helping them meet the many needs they can't yet fulfill on their own while supporting them as they try so determinedly to learn how to meet them themselves. If on top of all that parenting you add expectations about unschooling, it can get overwhelming.

Absolutely, if you're interested and curious, read and learn about unschooling. You'll find lots of ideas that will support your attachment parenting lifestyle, inspire your days, and excite you with thoughts about what the future holds. But feel free to remind yourself that right now, with your young children, you're "just parenting." And the great thing about attachment parenting is, if you do end up choosing unschooling for your child's learning environment, there won't be any difference in what your days look like before and after your child's "first day of compulsory schooling." It's living our lives together as a family.

Transitioning to Unschooling
with Young Children

Deschooling is that period of adjustment as your family moves from schooling to unschooling. Yet some parents discover unschooling before their children hit compulsory school age and don't send their kids at all. Though my oldest was almost ten and in grade four when we found homeschooling, my youngest was four and had only spent about six months in half-day junior kindergarten. Consequently, he had minimal deschooling to do—school attendance was a small, albeit annoying to him at the time, just a blip on his radar.

If you've been parenting in an attachment style, your young children can transition to an unschooling lifestyle easily. The days before and after your child's first day of compulsory schooling will look the same to them: they'll get up when they wake up, they'll play what they enjoy, they'll eat when they're hungry, you'll comfort them when they're upset, and they'll nap when (if?) they're tired.

Yet *your* thoughts may start to change—and it may take you by surprise. With attachment parenting you've been steadily moving away from a lot of conventional thinking related to parenting, and you've moved enough on the education front to have chosen to create an unschooling learning environment for your child. But with school now firmly in your thoughts, you'll likely discover pockets of conventional thinking about learning still tucked away in your mind. You may start to have more lofty goals for your newly school-aged child. You may find yourself looking for learning that looks more like school. That's not very surprising because it's likely what learning looks like to you. Remember that although your child hasn't been to school, you probably have. For many years.

When that happens, it's time for some more deschooling. I've mentioned before that parents continue to grow and learn about unschooling, and life, alongside their children—your learning is never "done." So don't knock yourself when it happens. These moments *will* pop up from time to time as you encounter new-to-you moments in your parenting journey. Just as having a child triggered you to examine and choose the kind of parents you want to be, your first child reaching school age is likely to uncover some conventional thoughts and assumptions about education you didn't realize you had. Same with other milestone moments, like when your eldest reaches the teen years. Conventional expectations about the transition to adulthood will probably begin to explode into your thoughts like popcorn.

What can you do? I think being mindful and aware of my thoughts has helped me catch my more knee-jerk reactions before injuries occur. For me, the idea isn't to reject ideas solely on the basis that they are conventional, but to catch thoughts and actions that are based mostly on the fact that "that's the way everyone does it." I want to think about and analyze the situations for myself and *choose* my path forward with my children.

So what are some of the conventional ideas about learning that may pop to mind as your child reaches an age when the educational system would start teaching them in earnest, expecting them to perform to a certain level?

- You may find yourself feeling an urge to start teaching your child instead of watching for learning.
- You may find yourself looking at their activities through a school filter, looking for school-like topics, like reading and math.
- You may find yourself feeling an urge to direct their play to more "respectable" activities.
- You may find yourself feeling an urge to sign them up for "lessons" without considering their interest, like art or swimming or those cool-looking homeschool field trips.
- You may find yourself looking for signs that their activities are more "purposeful," more goal-oriented.

Your triggers may be different, but if it happens, first take a couple deep breaths. A stressed mind finds it hard to think outside conventional lines. When you're feeling a bit more open, start digging into your thoughts about learning. Explore more deeply the principles of learning that underscore unschooling. Sure you may have read about them before, even intellectually agreed with them, but now you have a living and breathing child you love in front of you. It's time to mesh your theoretical understanding with the practice of living and learning with your child. Revisit those questions. What does real learning look like? When does the best learning happen? Can we really define what every person "should" know as they transition to the adult world? Is a timeline for learning a useful concept? How is it helpful that unschoolers develop their own unique web of learning connections?

And alongside that, as always, go back to looking at your child's perspective, their needs and wants. Instead of trying to direct them, use their interest as your guide. What are they doing? Why? Really look at them. Their learning doesn't look like worksheets and tests, but I bet they're learning. Their learning isn't necessarily "this is math" and "this is reading," but I bet it encompasses the much larger terrain of life. Life is full of numbers and letters *and* emotions and play and thinking and discovery and logic and movement and and and ... so many things!

Remember, it's *all* important.

And they have a lifetime to explore it.

Unschooling and the Power Paradigm

Most information I've come across about parenting, whether in conversations, online, in books and magazines, or through TV and movies, promotes an "us versus them" attitude: adults versus children. Even when it isn't mentioned explicitly, it's there. A quick web search turns up articles such as these from popular parenting sites: "Get Your Kid to Stay in Bed"; "15 Foods All Kids Should Eat"; "Don't Buy These Video Games"; "How to Deal with Defiant Kids"; "How to Keep Your Cool When Your Kids Push Your Buttons"; and "How to Deal With Your

Preteen's Messy Bedroom." As you read those headlines, can't you just feel the pervasive undercurrent of power struggles? Of pitting parents against their children?

What If You Don't Presume
Power Struggles Are Inevitable?

Moving away from the paradigm of adults versus children is really helpful in allowing unschooling to flourish. Why? Well, what are some of the things you begin doing more of as your family moves to unschooling? One would be moving away from telling your kids what to learn and focusing more on diving into what they find interesting. Another would be opening up everyday situations for further discussion and giving them more opportunity to make choices. Both of these are examples of moving away from adults exerting power over children to control them.

This can be thought of as us adults handing more power over to our children. And though that image is a step closer, it still leaves us with an image of "us and them"—just with the power slightly more balanced. That can be tricky to implement though, and sometimes parents can overcompensate. Giving the children more power than the adults in the family is not better—it can lead to children that feel entitled regardless of the situation.

What If We Remove the "Us and Them" Dichotomy As Well?

Instead of thinking of our relationships in terms of power management between parents and children, let's drop the age distinction altogether.

We don't need to drop the concept of power. After all, power is just a representation of what we can accomplish. To feel powerful is to feel strong and capable of action. What we can drop is the overtone of power *over* others. Most adults do feel more powerful than children because they have more experience and feel more capable in many situations. That's natural. But instead of using that power advantage to control our children, we can use it to work together as a family in support of each other.

What If We Envision Our Family As a Group—One Powerful Team?

Sure, the children will have less power to contribute, certainly when they are younger, but that's not a surprise, is it? They are children. It's not about everyone being equal; it's not about giving my children as much power as I have. It's about showing them how powerful we are when we all act *together*. Acting together in support of each other helps everyone in the family feel supported and loved; they feel safe because they have the power of their family behind them. Even when a child isn't able to contribute concretely towards a sibling's or parent's goal, they can still actively contribute by being emotionally supportive, and by not putting up barriers.

What do I mean by that? If a child feels powerless in a family, there's a good chance they will try to exert what little power they feel they do have to thwart others in reaching their goals: take away someone else's power to increase their own. Jill wants to play her video game? Adam might try to frustrate her in all sorts of ways: playing loudly in the room; running in front of the TV; tossing toys at her—all in an attempt to get an explosive reaction. The power in the air is almost tangible. These kinds of power struggles can play out over and over, day after day.

Remember though, when kids are younger this might happen innocently enough because younger Adam wants to play with Jill and doesn't yet realize that while trying to meet his needs, he's actively impeding hers. When parents see this happening they can engage Adam in other activities. Jill will appreciate the support in meeting her needs, and Adam gets and appreciates the attention and engagement he was looking for. And in short conversations and observations with Adam over time, he will begin to understand and incorporate the perspective of others. And during a quiet moment, explaining Adam's perspective to Jill will also help her better understand the situation (meaning that Adam's motivation isn't to frustrate her but to meet his wish to play).

Building that kind of supportive relationship with your children allows them to feel more comfortable in the family and to trust that their needs and wishes will be fully considered. From there, they don't feel the need to exert power over others—to feel powerful by frustrating others.

But what about when your children's needs are at cross-purposes? How might you go about working with them to find a path forward that supports everyone? What might it look like when we work together as a team, as a family?

Let's play with an example using some of my personal experience. If one of my children says they want to visit the science centre soon, I might say, "Let's go check out the calendar." Together (usually, or I'd look myself if they were busy) we'd see what days we are free in the next week or two (my kids are older now and often they'll check the calendar first before proposing plans). From the possibilities, we'd figure out if they have a preference, discussing that a bit so we could prioritize the available days.

Then I'd ask my other kids if they were interested in coming too. Note that I don't ask my child to ask their siblings—I figure out the family logistics in support of them. I have more experience with their different personalities and interests and can more quickly, and successfully, work out possibilities with them. Over the years they have all seen me in action countless times, figuring out plans, and definitely use that skill themselves now.

If everyone wanted to go, we'd have a quick discussion about which day, choose one, and mark it on the calendar. If one or more of the other kids didn't want to go, we'd keep digging. If they, and I, were comfortable with them staying home on their own, I'd confirm they were fine with that, and they'd look forward to having the run of the house while the rest of us looked forward to the science centre. When they were younger, I'd likely check with my husband to see if he was planning on working from home one day in the next week or so. Or we'd make it a weekend (usually more of a last resort because weekends are typically busier at attractions). Or I'd ask my mom if she'd like to come over and hang out with the stay-at-home child while the rest of us went. Or if she'd like to meet us there—sometimes the previously uninterested child was happy to come and spend some time with Grams. Sometimes one of the kids was less interested in the exhibits, but chose to come because the cafeteria pizza was surprisingly good and they wanted to eat lunch there. If that was the case, they'd bring their handheld games to play, or music to listen to while others explored the exhibits. Or maybe they were interested in the store and we'd plan to spend more than the usual amount of time in there during that particular visit.

My goodness, there are just so many ways it could go! So many ways it did go over the years. One thing that wasn't questioned though was somebody's wish to do something. Sure, somebody might ask why the other person wanted to do or not do something, and sometimes minds changed with further discussion, but doing our best in the end to meet anyone's wishes was a given.

I think the key was, and is, to keep an open mind and use the conversations with my children to incorporate their ideas; not to try to convince them to agree to any plan I had already formed in my head. If I'm listening politely and waiting for an opening to add a "but," then I'm not really hearing them. That's a clue to me that it's time to take a breath, or a break, or whatever helps me drop my preconceived solution, drop my urge to try to use my power to control the situation, and start fresh.

Another really interesting outcome I've seen is that children that feel fully supported, that feel the power of their family behind them, become much more discriminating in their wishes. Life isn't a constant barrage of I want this and this and this with little rhyme or reason. That doesn't mean I always understand why they want to do or have something, but that I trust they are motivated by a real need or want. Even if there were times over the years when their motivation may have been more frivolous, they saw me take their wishes seriously and do my best to meet them, and that built their trust in me.

Think of the reverse situation. If children are used to only some of their needs and wants being considered and fulfilled by their parents, they take that into consideration moving forward. They're smart! If they are used to, say, only one in five of their requests being taken seriously, they'll be sure to ask for five in hopes of getting at least one. And to get to those five, they may be asking for some things that would be fun, but aren't particularly necessary in their eyes. What is necessary is getting *something*. Some attention, some consideration, some feedback that says they are important. Some power. In that situation they can come across as needy because they always seem to be asking for something. That worries the parents and they may feel they need to say no more often so their child learns "they can't have everything," so the percentage of needs met falls even further, prompting the child to ask for more again, and so on. It can quickly become a downward spiral. From there, recovery of that trust and relationship may take a while, but it's definitely worth it.

Feeling powerful is, well, empowering! Imagine how wonderful your children will feel knowing they have the power of their family behind them. Tossing the parents versus kids attitude found in many parenting discussions and being careful not to use our power as parents over our children to control them, but rather to throw behind them and support them as they live and learn, will go a long way toward creating a joyful family atmosphere for both parents and kids that will last a lifetime.

How Do You Measure "Fair"?

The idea behind fairness is an important one: to be fair is to be free from bias. In families that means not showing favour for one child over another. It has come to symbolize love. And parents don't want any of their children to feel they are less loved than their sibling(s).

But how do you measure "fair"?

Most conventional families measure it based on quantity. They strive for equality: they give all their children the same number of gifts for holidays; or spend the same amount of money on each for their birthdays; or sign them up for the same number of recreational activities.

Is that fair? It certainly looks so from the parents' point of view, "Look, the numbers prove it!" And over time, the kids hear the message loud and clear and start to view their lives through the same filter—everything is weighed and measured. "Hey, his bowl of ice cream is bigger than mine!" "Why can't I go out with my friends? She went last night!" Parents can cling to this equality justification, but the scorekeeping gets wearying. In the end, it doesn't really seem like a helpful measure of love, does it?

So how else might we look at things?

Unschooling families are more apt to observe and evaluate situations from the *child*'s perspective. Sure, both kids got a pair of skates, but did they both *want* a pair of skates? As parents move to unschooling they begin to see fairness not as a quantitative measure of what the parents give, but as a qualitative measure of the value each child receives. They no longer ask themselves, "Do *I* think my children should feel loved and secure?" They ask, "Do *they* feel loved and secure?"

Equality in what you give each child isn't a helpful measure of fairness or love because what each child needs from you is likely to be different. One child may need more of your time, wanting a lot of personal interaction. Another might have an active outside interest that needs more of the family's money to support it. Still another might need more of your active participation, joining them as they pursue their interests. You may be giving each of your children very different things that take varying amounts of time and effort and money. But when their needs are met, they each feel content, secure, and happy: equally loved.

Yet no matter how hard you try, there may be real reasons why things feel unfair to a child in the moment. Maybe one child gets sick or injured and needs more attention for a while. Maybe there's a busy season with one child's activity. Siblings can understand the need, but still feel things are unfair in the moment. Those are really good moments to talk with your child about the situation. Or better yet, just focus on listening. Hear their perspective and acknowledge it. Be compassionate. If it seems appropriate, share your perspective—though not with an eye to convince them to change their feelings. You're learning more about each other. About life. That's why I don't see eye to eye with those who feel parents shouldn't help their children as much as possible because kids need to learn that "life isn't fair." There will be enough real moments when life feels unfair—we don't need to manufacture them.

An interesting outcome I've observed is that when each child feels like their needs are being met and life feels fair, they feel less competitive with their siblings. There's minimal push and pull and struggle for attention or power. That's because they come to measure their happiness based on their own needs being met, not constantly looking to those around them for validation of their own worth.

If their sibling gets a *insert fun thing* and is really happy? They don't feel spiteful; they don't demand they get one too just to be fair. That's not to say they might not try it out and like it and ask for one too because they feel they would enjoy it. If so, when they get it they'll probably use it and learn and expand their world. But if they want it just because their sibling has it, once they get it, their mission is accomplished and there's no need to actually use it—it just sits on the shelf. What a different mindset!

Instead of learning to measure fairness through numbers, they learn to see and consider the real people behind the numbers. They learn people have different needs, and that it's meeting those needs that is important, not necessarily how those needs are met. As they extend this understanding beyond their family, their friends feel better understood and supported. That's much better information to bring into adulthood than a penchant for tit-for-tat comparisons.

Value and love in a family isn't best measured by everything being equal. It's better to look to your children and see if *they* feel like a valued and cared for member of the family. If not, start there.

Communication instead of Discipline

Discipline. It's a word with multiple meanings and its interpretation often depends on your personal experiences and world view.

I like to think of discipline as an "activity, exercise, or a regimen that develops or improves a skill; training: A daily stint at the typewriter is excellent discipline for a writer." I'm pretty transparent that way—I usually lean toward the meaning that supports real learning.

But, certainly in mainstream conversations about children and discipline, the word is more likely to mean "punishment or penalty in order to train and control; correct; or chastise" or, a bit more sinisterly, "systematic training in obedience to regulations and authority." (Thanks, dictionary.com!)

Choosing our approach to discipline is a significant aspect of parenting. A quick web search on ways to discipline children brings up methods such as physical punishment (like spanking), emotional punishment (like taking a valued toy or activity away), consequences (like losing a related privilege), expressing disapproval (making the parent's love conditional), etc. These are all examples of adults exerting their power over children in an effort to control their behaviour.

Leaving aside the incredible damage these methods can do to the parent-child relationship, why are these methods rather ineffective, certainly in the long term? Because these punitive actions do not help the child understand the reason why the behaviour is frowned upon; they merely teach the child that the parent doesn't like it. The threat of punishment may motivate the child to avoid that behaviour when the parent is around, but it doesn't help them appreciate why they may want to rethink those actions in their day-to-day lives. These methods train, they don't explain. Discipline keeps the focus on the surface level of behaviour: do this; don't do that. Or else.

So let's dig deeper. What drives behaviour? One of the main motivators is character. Our character, the traits that define us as unique people, are what we draw on when choosing our actions.

We aren't trying to train our children how to behave so we don't need to discipline or control our children to coerce them to stay on our narrow path. Instead, we are helping our children learn about character; about the range of options we all have regarding how we choose to behave. And how do unschooling kids learn best? Through experience. And how do we best support their learning? Through conversations. Help your children experience the situations they are drawn to, brief them on what they can expect to happen, and then have conversations with them to help them process the experience—debrief. Talk about the situations that arose, about how they saw things, about our own experiences, about ways a person might act or react, about how things might move forward.

Open, honest, and clear communication best supports our goal of helping them learn about character, about discovering the person they want to be. When things don't go well, instead of disciplining, i.e., punishing them for behaviour that's already happened, focus on the future—help them figure out what other choices they have available to them for the next time a similar situation arises. And depending on the child, these might be longer conversations as you're both curled up on the couch, banter around the kitchen counter, a chat in the car, or a few words exchanged here and there as inspiration hits.

I want to take a moment to touch on the idea of positive discipline. The ideas and tools they suggest focus more on the parent-child relationship over punishment and emphasize working together with your child. They are definitely a great step forward. But there are still complications that can arise. Let's take a look at the idea of "natural consequences" for example. They are described as the consequences that happen when no adult interferes in the situation. That sounds pretty reasonable, doesn't it? No punishment, just experience?

It does seem logical, but I prefer to call that just plain living. It's life. Things don't always go as planned or hoped for—shit happens. But in my experience, taking those moments and calling them "natural consequences" tempts parents to purposely stand back and not help out, to not lend their experience to facilitate a situation—all in the name of their child learning a lesson. The parents deem the lesson more important than whatever the child was trying to accomplish. That doesn't seem natural. There are enough times when I truly don't have the experience, influence, or skill to be able to help a situation that I don't have to artificially manufacture them. I can do my very best and life still happens, not fairy tales.

One of the benefits of focusing on helping our unschooling kids learn about themselves and develop their unique character is that as they get older, they better understand themselves and the kind of person they want to be, and the easier it becomes for them to make real choices about their behaviour. Not muddied by reactionary motivations like rebellion, their choices don't change depending on who's around to see. One of the common traits of unschooling teens is that they don't have two different personas: one for peers and one for adults. They get to just be themselves.

As unschoolers, we are focused on supporting our kids as they learn through living. We help them discover themselves and the person they want to be, rather than trying to mould them into our version of the "ideal" child. And our parenting choices are all in support of that. Punishment, discipline, demands—they all interfere with that learning. Instead, we talk with our children as people, as human beings and figure out ways we can best help them move forward contentedly with their day, their week, their life.

A Bigger Picture: The Transition from Childhood to Adolescence

The timing of the transition from childhood to adolescence is not the same for all children, though typically it's somewhere in the range of eight to twelve years old. There are lots of factors that can influence this, from their own personality and emotional growth patterns, to having older siblings (introducing teen topics into the family earlier), to the age of those whose company the child naturally enjoys, to the physical onset of puberty.

Regardless of their age, it's a time when an unschooling child may be feeling unsettled and introspective as they ponder the transition from child to teen. They may find their enthusiasm for childhood loves waning, while at the same time still be casting about for new passions to catch their interest. A time of flux. It's also a time when the child's perspective grows to encompass more of the world and they begin to contemplate their place in it, often with broadening social interests and needs.

This transition can be a bit unsettling for parents too. They have watched their child devour information over the past few years, their seemingly insatiable learning pretty transparent—the evidence is often all over the house! Even if they aren't learning the same things as conventionally schooled children, the learning is obvious and parents have probably developed a pretty comfortable routine of support: they're quite adept at finding supplies to support their child's ongoing interests; they have sources for finding new things they might enjoy; and the family has favourite places to visit regularly, like parks or museums or the store at the science centre. Yet now they may be discovering that this routine is losing its lustre for their child.

The conventional description of this transition time, nowadays called "tween" (an amalgamation of "inbetween" and "teen", because humans like to label things), is that they are too old for kid stuff and too young for teen stuff. But with unschooling we don't really make age-related declarations. We don't define things as "too young" or "too old," instead we support our child's exploration—they are where they are. I'm also not a big fan of the way the term "tween" is bandied about in lists of what they'll like and not like, because it seems to diminish the real work they are doing. They are honing their sense of self, contemplating the kind of person they want to be, nurturing dreams of the future and wondering how they might find their niche in the adult world. It's no longer mostly about the facts of the world and clear distinctions— right/wrong, yes/no—but increasingly about their emotional development and growth. They begin to explore moral questions, develop empathy, and generally, see a bigger picture of the world.

It's also a time when they may become interested in exploring that world more on their own. If that's the case, help them find ways they can test the edges of their comfort zone while still having a backup plan that gives you both a measure of reassurance. Going to a movie on their own or with friends. Hanging on their own in town for a couple hours. A hike in the park. Visiting out-of-town friends for a few days. Help them find ways to explore their budding independence, maybe with a cell phone in tow, just in case plans change on the fly. And don't be surprised if this skirts your comfort zones as well. Your child is growing up! But remember, you're also growing and learning alongside them. Work through it together.

You can take the same tack if their interest in exploring social relationships or group activities grows: help them find good matches and support their drive for more independence. Another striking development is that conversations will become even more interesting as their analysis of situations expands and they incorporate more of the perspective of others. Their ideas will be more all-encompassing, branching out in new and fascinating directions.

What if they become drawn to quieter activities during this time? In my experience, ages eight to nine stand out as a time when some unschooling parents notice their boys become more withdrawn and contemplative. That's cool too! Everyone will have their own ways of processing and learning and growing. In this case, I would remind you to check in with them regularly—find time to sit with them while they are doing their thing, maybe sharing their shows, or their game, or their books, leaving a relaxed and easy opening for conversation if they're interested. It can be tempting to just leave them be, especially if you are busy meeting the needs of younger siblings, but it's important to keep your connection with them strong, even as it begins to look different.

And really, what's important no matter which path they take through this time, nor how often they choose to switch it up, is to keep your relationship connected and strong. Be sure to listen to them whenever they want to talk, or bat ideas around with them if that's what they like. Or even just *be* with them, in the stillness and quiet. It lets them truly know you are there whenever they need you. It gives them the time and space to choose to open up conversations, or to sink into the comfort of your company. Remember, you're supporting them as they explore their expanding world, and their expanding selves—as they live their life.

Teens Reap what Their Parents Sow

Teenagers. What's the first thing that pops to mind? Something reminiscent of the My Chemical Romance song? "Teenagers scare the living shit out of me." A quick web search reveals that the conventional wisdom surrounding the teenage years is mainly focused on helping parents survive this inevitably challenging stage. Mainstream society treats it as a foregone conclusion—a belief as strong as tomorrow they'll be a day older. This stage of parent-child relationship discord is practically seen as a rite of passage.

But what if it's the conventional wisdom surrounding raising children that is specifically setting teens up for this additional turmoil, beyond the physical and emotional changes that adolescence brings? What if we take a different tack? What if parents work to support rather than control their teens? What if we don't try to keep them away from adult society as long as possible? And from their perspective, what if a teen's desire for more independence and responsibility isn't met by a wall of resistance?

Unschooling families are giving it a shot. In essence, they choose to avoid the power and authority dynamic that many families set up at home. Without the "us versus them" mentality, unschooling teens don't have a "parental authority" they have to challenge to get permission to do many things. Instead, they know their parents will *help* them as they pursue their independence and journey into adulthood. What a thoroughly divergent perspective from which to enter your teen years!

Teens Growing Independence

In more conventional families, where teens are less supported and more controlled, many teens are compelled to pursue their growing independence out from under the watchful and judgmental eyes of parents. Adults know this, but instead of reciprocating with real life opportunities, many towns and cities actively resist: some are raising the compulsory school age so they remain housed in schools longer (my province did this a few years ago, from sixteen to eighteen); some have instituted youth curfews so the police can keep them out of the community at large; public places like malls have created additional security measures and regulations designed to keep teens spending or out. It seems we are doing our best to shut teens out of, instead of welcoming them into, adult society.

How does this look different in unschooling families? Instead of creating an uncomfortable environment at home from which teens are eager to escape, they cultivate a loving and supportive one (supportive of the *teen's* goals). On top of that, unschooling parents support their child's wishes to get together with other teens. They'll open up their home and provide a fun environment for the teens to hang out. Movies? Snacks? Sleeping bags? A cozy and welcoming room in which to relax and chat late into the night? Unschooling parents have developed strong and connected relationships with their teens and talk openly with them, figuring out what they want to do, and working together to help them accomplish it. What if their teen wants to visit others? They help out by driving (maybe hours away), or making other arrangements like bus tickets, or even flights. Instead of fearing teens gathering, unschooling parents help make it happen and create accommodating environments in which the teens can enjoy themselves. And in that enjoyment, they are learning so much.

Joining Adult Society

The conventional educational paradigm says that children go to school to learn what they need to know so they can graduate into adult society. For its part, society seems to be doing its best to shut teens out of the "real world" until that magical graduation day. And then we expect them to smoothly jump right in to this new world and navigate it successfully.

What are unschooling parents doing instead? Creating a learning environment for their children that is based in the real world from the get-go. They support their teenager's interest in engaging with society at large—whatever it looks like and at whatever age it develops. They help them find opportunities to volunteer in areas of interest; seek mentors to help them pursue their passions even more deeply; drive them to jobs; support them if they want to learn to drive themselves. In other words, they help their teens find opportunities to participate in adult society *now*, as much and as deeply as they are interested in.

The Family Atmosphere Parents Choose to Sow

When conventional parents choose to create a relationship with their children that is adversarial in nature that's probably what they'll get in return as their children become teens and begin to exercise their growing autonomy. It shouldn't be surprising that if it's tools of control they have seen from their parents, those are the tools they will reach for in conflict. You can only harvest what is planted.

Unschoolers choose to plant different seeds. Instead of seeing themselves as directing their teens with an attitude of "I always know better," unschooling parents see themselves as supporting their child along the road that the *teen* is choosing. Supporting them means sharing our experiences, knowledge, and thoughts, but not directing their path. We're available for conversations whenever our teen strikes one up; we initiate them as moments arise; and let them end naturally, instead of forcing them to continue to "make a point." We treat them as the intelligent beings they are.

I have found that my involvement in my teens' lives has not become fraught with conflict; but it does look different as they get older. I'm less involved with their direct learning—helping them find answers to their questions, helping them get their day-to-day needs met—and more involved with helping them navigate their journey into adulthood. We chat about longer term goals and the various ways to meet them; relationships and the motivations and needs of others; and figure out plans as they explore the world farther afield. I treasure our relationships.

In unschooling families, the teenage years, though still full of the twists and turns and angst of life, are not further complicated by the conventional assumption that teens are troublesome and rebellious and need to be controlled. Unschooled teens have been living in and observing the real world for years and, with the loving support of their parents, know when they are ready to move more directly into adult society, whatever their age.

CHAPTER FIVE

:: relationships ::

What do relationships look like through the lens of unschooling?

The World of Siblings and Unschooling

I've received some questions from readers about supporting siblings with differing needs and interests and sibling relationships, so I thought I'd address them together (I've paraphrased so they are anonymous). A couple of them also have extenuating circumstances—I'll talk about those bits up front.

What are some tips for making things work when you have four kids that are so close in age and are all very strong willed.

Would love to see the topic of siblings/meeting different needs discussed.

How, as a mom of six children, do I spend time engaged with each of my children's passions? All of their interests are different, I have been feeling guilty lately that I am not fully engaging with any of my children and how do I be right there for them and have a clean house?

The clean house issue is wrapped up in this one. It's pretty clear that mom's feeling a sharp either/or distinction: being with and supporting her children vs a clean house. One thing that might help break out of that dichotomy is to move away from the mindset that these are mutually exclusive activities.

If this is the case for you, try going about your day from that new perspective and see what comes up. Are there moments when you can, say, tidy up a bit while you're chatting with a child or two? Or fold laundry on the bed with a young one or two, covering them in warm towels? I have quite a few pictures of my kids when they were little wrapped up in laundry, or using the laundry basket as a boat. Or a hat. How about emptying the dishwasher while they're playing a game at the kitchen table? Look for ways things can be combined, instead of feeling like you're doing one at the expense of the other. It's amazing what a few minutes here and there can do.

I'd love to hear more regarding your perspective on sibling rivalry, conflict, etc. No matter how I've tried, my two older children fight terribly, about 50 percent of the time. I started unschooling my son recently while my daughter attends a Waldorf school—she does not want to be homeschooled.

Here there's the overlay of one child attending school—that can definitely add extra strain to the sibling dynamics if they judge each other negatively for their choices. You'll probably need to help them work through that tangle. As moments of conversation arise, you might share one of the reasons behind their sibling's choices, helping each better understand the other.

Now let's examine some ideas about supporting the interests and passions of multiple children and navigating sibling relationships. First, let's look at a couple of real life parameters to help give this discussion some perspective:

1. There are only twenty-four hours in a day. This means that the more children you have, the less time you have available to spend with them individually. That's not to make anyone feel bad for having multiple children! The joy of a houseful of children can be immense. But I remember having three children ages five and under—it's busy! There are a lot of practical needs that need to be attended to. That's just a reality you've chosen for a few years.

2. Choosing unschooling for your family doesn't mean life will be "perfect." Don't expect that everyone will be happy all the time and that siblings will be the best of friends. We are all real people. We all have different per-

sonalities and needs and dreams, which may or may not mesh very well with those of the people we happen to live with. And just because we choose what we do in the moment, doesn't mean things always flow smoothly—many things are out of our control.

All that said, unschooling is a wonderful environment in which to support our children and our family relationships, now and in the longer-term.

Supporting Everyone's Interests and Needs

This can definitely be challenging, getting more and more complicated as more personalities are added to the mix. Maybe some want to go out places; others prefer to stay home. Maybe some love to run around at the playground; others prefer indoor attractions. Maybe none like the grocery store. Try something, see how it goes, talk about it, and work together to adjust the plan accordingly. Try again. Mix things up to see what happens. Think outside that box. Is grocery shopping an incredible challenge every week? Look at online shopping and delivery—is it really as expensive as you think? Find out. The more facts you have to work with, the better. Keep trying.

How the members of the family interact isn't something that has one "right answer"—it's a process. And remember, things change over time: interests change, circumstances change, their independence grows, etc. Even if things have been going pretty smoothly for a while, they will change. Play and tweak and try things out. Together. Always work with those involved.

One thing I found really helpful when the kids were younger and we were trying to figure out a plan for something, was to talk to each of them individually, giving each of them my focused attention. I'd find out why they did or did not want to do X. If they didn't, I'd ask if they were amenable to X-Y, a modified version of X (that modification may be my idea or one of their sibling's). I'd ask for their ideas. Then chatting with the next child, I could quickly explain their sibling's point of view (helping them learn about each other) and how they felt about it. Even if it took a number of chats (usually pretty short), over a few days, back and forth with each child, I'd get a clearer picture of what each of their needs and wishes were and most often we could find something that would work for everyone involved. Sometimes the plans got quite elaborate. We were all learning.

With this process, not only do the children feel heard and understood, but they also have time and space to think. Especially for quieter personalities, ones who may be uncomfortable when expected to speak up and think on the spot, group decision making can be challenging. Ease into that when it seems appropriate. Sometimes, when I thought there would be general agreement, I would bring up the plans when we were altogether and we'd work through the details. More learning. Their abilities to analyze situations, consider everyone's needs, and find workable paths forward grew steadily.

And remember, you don't need to do it all on your own. Maybe with young kids another pair of hands around the house will help—maybe a mother's helper, maybe a neighbourhood teen who enjoys playing with kids. Maybe one child really enjoys spending a day with their grandparents every week or two. Maybe adding their friends to the mix, at home or out and about, helps make the dynamics more manageable for a few hours. Experiment. Play. When things go awry, it's not the end of the world, try something else next time. Try to be light and nimble and considerate. Learn.

This process is about developing their trust in *you*. And the result is a strong, connected relationship with each of your children.

Sibling Relationships and Conflict

Do you have the expectation that your children should get along? If so, why? Because they live in the same house? Share the same genetic soup? That seems a stretch. On the other hand, everyone wants to feel safe in their own home. Even better, to feel understood and supported. Sometimes we can feel like as parents our foremost goal is to minimize conflict between our children ("don't fight with your brother"), but that's more about treating the symptoms rather than the cause. Instead, think of these interactions as part of a journey in which we're learning ways to live comfortably with the other members of our family. From that level of comfort, conflict arises less and less. And when it does, those involved have helpful tools to move through it more smoothly.

Here are a few ideas for parents that, in my experience, can help families take that journey together.

First, when conflicts arise, don't insist that your children talk to each other to "work it out." That conversation will be about meeting *your* needs, not theirs. Take your expectations out of the mix. Talk to each of them individually. See the situation from their perspective. If you don't understand, keep trying. They have their perspective and their reasons. When you deeply understand and empathize with each of your children, you'll likely be in a better position to help them find workable paths through their conflicts.

Second, shift away from the conventional power paradigm, where family relationships are seen in terms of a power dynamic—both adults versus children, and children amongst themselves. In that environment, actions are motivated by a need to gain power *over* others, to fight for or defend their position in the family hierarchy. You can start by moving away from the adults versus children model. Instead of using your power to try to get them to do what you want them to do, support them as *they* explore the world. As the power struggles fade between parents and children, the children begin to see how powerful the family is when they actively *support* each other. Everyone feels safer because they have the power of their family behind them. They no longer need to feel powerful by frustrating their siblings—by exerting power *over* them. There is less and less driving need or reason to create conflict.

And third, look at how you measure "fair" between siblings. Conventionally, many families measure it based on quantity and equate "fair" with "equal": the same number of gifts for holidays, the same number of outside activities, etc. Over time, the kids hear the message loud and clear and start to view their lives through that same filter: "He had three cookies—I only got two!" Moving to unschooling helps us begin to see fairness not as a quantitative measure of what the parents give, but as a qualitative measure of the value each child receives. That's a helpful shift because what each child needs from you is probably different. One may need more of your time, another more money for their outside interests, and another more of your direct participation in their activities. You may be giving each of your children very different things that take varying amounts of time and effort and money, but when their unique needs are being met, they each feel content, secure, and happy.

When we support and celebrate each of our children as the unique individuals they are, we better foster a family atmosphere of joy, harmony, and safety from which minimal conflict grows.

Building Strong Relationships
with Your Kids

Are you feeling disconnected from one or more of your children? Or are you a working parent wanting to build a deeper relationship with your kids? Or a step-parent wanting to create solid relationships with your step-children?

A relationship is defined as a connection between two people, whether by blood, marriage, or emotion. It's a rather perfunctory relationship that is built on blood only. Building a meaningful relationship means *emotionally* connecting with the other person, getting to know and understand them. In a well-connected relationship between parent and child there is a beautiful give-and-take and flow, a high level of trust, and genuine respect. And in any relationship *you* want to build stronger, it is up to you to make the first move. So what can you do?

There are a couple of things that I often see get in the way when a parent is trying to connect/reconnect with a child and build a stronger relationship. The first is the parent is not honestly evaluating how supportive they are of connecting opportunities when they appear. Think about the flow of your relationship with your children as it sits right now. When they ask you for help do you most often say yes? Do you consistently help right away or put them off until it's more convenient for you, if ever? Maybe they've stopped asking for your help except as a last resort? Or does your spouse often ask you for help for them? Looking at these questions can help you see the signals you are giving them regarding your availability for connection. Each of these situations, if they occur with any regularity, interferes with the healthy give-and-take of a relationship.

Let's look at the flow from the other direction. When you ask your child for help is the answer most often no? Are the answers to your general questions short and sweet, lacking the richer details that deepen an already well-connected relationship? These are clues that your child may be feeling disconnected too.

The second thing I see time and again is the parent trying to connect with their child by attempting to pull the child to them, rather than going to the child: "Want to go for a bike ride with me?" The answer is often no because as part of the relationship disconnect they may not trust that you are suggesting the activity for their enjoyment. And are you really? Do you truly think it is something your child would enjoy, or is it really something that *you* would enjoy doing with them? There's an incredibly important difference there.

How can you break this cycle? For the next while, just stop asking. You already know you are both feeling disconnected so stop creating moments that highlight this disconnect and increase frustration in the relationship. Stop asking questions where the answer is likely to be no or lacking in any meaningful detail.

So, if you're not asking questions, not asking for help, not asking them to join you in activities, what do you do instead? Go to them; join your children in activities they enjoy. Take the time to see the world through their eyes. Spend some time quietly observing them so you start to see what kinds of things they like to do. Make getting to know them one of your high priority projects. Watch the TV shows and movies they like *with* them. No need to make conversation to connect; your relaxed presence is a starting point for building future connections. Let them just get used to your company. Maybe play their favourite board or video games with them. If they don't yet want you to play with them, don't take it personally; sit nearby and soak up their joy. Take your direction from them.

But don't do these things passively; passionately spend this time observing and learning more about them. Creating a strong base of trust to build a relationship on is not about putting in time with your child but about using that time to actually learn who your child is: the activities they enjoy, the food they like to eat, the kinds of clothes they prefer to wear. What are the signs that they are hungry or tired? What kind of humour do they enjoy? Do they have a favourite seat by the TV? Do they like to go out and about regularly or do they prefer spending time at home?

If your child doesn't like apples, don't continue to offer them apples. Offer up their favourite seat if they come to watch TV and you happen to be sitting there. Offer to take them to the park regularly if you know they like to go; and don't if you learn they don't. Don't offer advice while playing games together if you know they don't like that. Bring them their favourite snack, or pick them up a T-shirt you're quite sure they'll like as an impromptu gift. Show them that you understand *them*. To build a relationship with your child is to connect with them as they truly are, not with an idealized version you have in your mind.

In that same vein, don't just imagine what a great relationship looks like to you and start acting like it already exists. That's presumptuous. Even though your internal motivation has changed, your child can't see that; your actions can still look selfish from their current perspective. You need to *show* them and earn their trust—no short cuts.

And a quick note—if you are a working or newer-to-their-lives parent with a spouse that already has a strong relationship with the child, these ideas aren't about trying to create the same relationship with your child or stepchild or grandchild that they have—it's about creating a strong base of trust from which your unique relationship with your child can grow.

Once you begin to deeply understand your child you can begin to connect with them where *they* are—that is the comfortable place from which they can welcome you. And once you know your child well, you will be able to bring things to them that they will be much more likely to enjoy with you. And that's a true connection: proof that you see *them*, that you understand who they really are.

As you create more and more of these connections your relationship will get stronger. And as you understand your children better, you will see that their actions and reactions are truly grounded in who they are, not random outbursts designed to frustrate you. As you understand their actions better you will be less frustrated and more trusting of them. And with this developing trust comes true respect, a deep sense of the inherent worth of your children, which will most likely be reciprocated in abundance as you use this strong base to build uniquely wonderful relationships together.

Have fun!

Exploring Relationships

Supporting our children as they learn about themselves and explore how they relate to others will help them immensely as they get older and interact more and more with the world at large.

Note that gaining experience with relationships doesn't necessarily mean interacting with lots of people. In fact, discovering how many people and relationships they are comfortable managing in their lives at any given time is an integral part of this process. There is no right or wrong answer—it's part of their personality, their individual makeup. They may revel in their time alone, or in spending lots of time in the company of others. Sometimes they may be looking to expand their connections with others; other times they may be looking to cocoon, to be with their own thoughts. And there's all points between. No matter, it's fine. It's great! Understanding and being comfortable *with themselves* is what's important. The number of friends or acquaintances a person has is not a useful measure of them as a human being.

And not only is this place of comfort with ourselves a wonderful place to be, it's also from this place that we feel most capable of stretching ourselves, of exploring our boundaries and discovering something new—learning. So, how can we support our children as they explore relationships?

By being a responsive partner to your child as they piece together how *they* like to engage with the world around them. For example, as you help them pursue their interests, explore different social environments with them: from one-on-one, to small gatherings, to large groups. Find appealing opportunities and offer them—people often gather around shared interests, from local clubs of a handful of people to large-scale conventions. If your child isn't interested at the time, don't worry, it's enough for them to know that these opportunities exist in the world. Expanding their world doesn't necessarily mean they have to personally experience everything: pictures of the continent on the other side of the world, or of the moon broaden their understanding and knowledge; as does listening to recordings of bird sounds or ocean waves; as does knowing there are philharmonic orchestra performances and comic book conventions and karate dojos nearby, if and when they're interested. And they have a lifetime to be interested.

Through this exploration, maybe they discover large groups overwhelm them right now. Or excite them. Maybe they find them tolerable when the reason for the gathering is near and dear to their heart. Explore one-on-one relationships—if they find another child they'd like to spend more time with, invite them over to visit regularly. Or be willing to take your child to visit them. Or meet them at other places, like a park or a museum, if that works out better.

All the while, conversations will come up. Emotional topics can be challenging, but don't dodge them. Chat with your child about their relationships: their feelings when things go awry; reasons why their friend might be acting certain ways; how other households and families function. Even if your child strongly prefers the company of his family, opportunities will arise for these kinds of conversations, not only through your family interactions, but also through TV shows, movies, books, online exchanges, and extended family gatherings.

Whatever your child's preference for relationship connections, large numbers or small, it probably won't change drastically as they get older, so it's most useful to help them understand and be comfortable with however that looks for them and gain experience engaging with the world from *that* perspective. That's valuable learning. If ever you are feeling unsure, wondering about their social interactions, look to them: are *they* comfortable with the relationships in their lives? Sure, dig into your thoughts and understand why you are feeling uncomfortable—that's your learning about yourself. But then shift and see the world through *their* eyes, and help them explore their thoughts and experiences. Support their learning.

Unschooling parents appreciate the value of supporting our children as they explore relationships. That learning is as valuable as any factual knowledge. Understanding themselves and how they relate with others will help them throughout their lifetime. They will be able to take it into consideration not only in their personal relationships, but in pursuing career and/or job opportunities as well, like choosing compatible work environments and managing relationships with co-workers.

Relationships are a fundamental piece of the being human puzzle. Conventionally, parents have one way of relating to their friends and colleagues and another way of relating to their children. The beauty of the relationships developed in unschooling families is that we don't treat people differently based on their age, so what our children learn about relationships growing up will always be helpful. Certainly the topics we chat about and the language we use evolve as they get older, but how we relate to each other as people, honestly and respectfully, doesn't change—from childhood, through the teenage years, to adulthood. The strong and trusting relationships I've developed with my children over the years are a wonderful foundation for their learning—and for our lives—together.

Finding Friends

When we get past the first impressions of unschooling as "crazy," often the next stage is seeing it as almost utopian. What a wonderful way of life for our children: diving into what interests them; enthusiastic yeses to their requests as often as feasible; strong and connected family relationships where their voice is heard and fully considered, etc.

And it *is* wonderful! But does it mean their life is perfect? Not by any stretch of the imagination.

As we spend more and more time with unschooling we begin to see it more clearly for what it is: life. Real life, with all its twists and turns and ups and downs. As unschooling parents we do our best to help our children's lives align as closely as possible to their goals and aspirations, but as they get older it inevitably dawns on us that things aren't always within our control.

Let's explore one such question I've seen come up pretty regularly in the lives of unschooling kids over the years: finding friends.

It can be challenging to support our children as they explore ways to work through these realities. We don't like to see our children sad or upset. We wish we could fix it for them, or somehow convince them not to be sad about it, but reality has its own timetable. And looking back, we come to realize that the skills our children learn as we help them explore ways to approach these kinds of situations, help them better weather the storm the next time it happens, and the next.

On the topic of finding friends, there are three things I'd encourage you to consider before you dive into conversations with your children.

First, if you find yourself ruminating about your children and the quantity/quality of their friendships, first check that it's a concern of *theirs*, not just of yours. Sometimes unschooling kids are happily immersed in their world, maybe with a couple of siblings, maybe with a friend they see irregularly. If the concern is specifically yours, that's a whole different conversation. For our purposes here, let's assume it's the *child* who is wishing to find more friends.

Next, let's take a moment to note that this question is *unrelated* to conventional society's ongoing concern with socialization and home/unschooling. There's a big difference between socialization and being social; between "acquiring the social skills appropriate to their social position" (dictionary.com) and hanging out with friends. Unschooling parents are pretty quickly comfortable with the idea that school is *not* a great place to learn social skills. But might it be a good place to find friends? Maybe.

Yet one thing's pretty certain, if you mention to a more conventional friend or family member that your child has been wanting to find more friends, in my experience, the most likely suggestion you're going to get is to send them to school—along with a helping of guilt that you've been depriving them of friends up to this point by keeping them home. Heck, that may be where your mind goes first too! And that's not very surprising—we've been well-trained. (This is as good a time as any to remind you that even if you think you "finished" deschooling long ago, I can almost guarantee that as new situations arise over the years you will excavate more pockets of conventional thinking to be examined. Or maybe I'm the only one?)

And that brings us to the third thing to contemplate: Is this really an unschooling question? Or is it a human question?

Think back to your days in school. Did you have a lot of friends? How many close friendships? Did you feel connected to the kids around you? Did you have much time to be social during school hours?

In reality, many school kids are lonely too. If school is "the answer" to the question of finding friends, how can that be? It doesn't make sense. Our experience—and even the conventional stories told through books and TV shows and movies—tell us that having lots of kids around in no way guarantees that solid friendships will develop.

Friendships are about connections, about finding common ground. At school, kids are gathered through shared geography and lumped together in classrooms by age. There's definitely a concentration of kids! Yet living in the same neighbourhood is a pretty weak connection upon which to build a friendship. Shared interests can definitely be a stronger starting point, but still no guarantee.

When our children express a wish to find friends we can do our best to help them pursue their desire for more connections. We can brainstorm ideas for finding and making connections (what group activities relate to their interests?). We can support them emotionally by commiserating with them about the mismatch between their reality and their vision surrounding friends. We can support them physically by inviting people into our homes (host a gaming day, a Lego party, etc.) and driving our children places. We can do our best to create an abundance of possibilities, but we can't control the outcomes.

We can encourage them to be open to other ways connect with people, ways that may not be their first choice but that may surprise them if they give them a shot, like online communities or conventions. We really can't predict where or when a connection might spark. We can validate, and yet accept, their disappointment. If we react too deeply, if we take on their sadness as our own, we risk sending the message this disappointment is a *bad thing*, a failure. It's not. Life is disappointing sometimes. We can keep going.

We can share our stories. I have a few close friends that I initially connected with through unschooling, while others remain lovely acquaintances. In contrast, the friends I had in school dropped away quickly once we left school: we didn't have enough connections outside of school to sustain the relationships. That's all okay—that's life. My daughter has made friends through Girl Guides, through volunteering, and through her interest in photography. Some have faded, others have blossomed. My son has a great group of friends right now at his dojo. But over the years one thing we've discovered is that the friendships we make aren't always in sync with our desire for friendship.

Seeing that bigger picture, that ebb and flow over the years, helps both us and our children be more patient with, and open to, the complexities of life. Through it all we support our children as they explore the ways in which they enjoy connecting with people, as they play with how much time they want to spend cultivating relationships—in number and in depth. It's an ongoing conversation. It's living. It's unschooling.

Online Connections: Do They Count?

Let's look at the scenario where your child is happy with their level of social interactions, yet you're feeling uncomfortable because the majority of your child's social interactions are online. Our children are growing up with online technology. It's more intuitive for them, so it can often be us parents who are concerned, while they are happily chatting with other kids in different time zones. Do online relationships really count?

Whenever I find myself uncomfortable with something in our unschooling lives, *why* is my favourite question. I keep asking it until I manage to unearth the root of the issue for me. Once I'm there, I can begin to make useful observations.

With our world becoming more and more connected through technology, online connections are becoming more commonplace, and more meaningful. Yet they are still often considered "less than." We tag our in-person encounters as IRL—in real life—as if our online connections aren't real. Why? In my experience, I often feel *more* connected to my online friends because we communicate more—both more often and in more depth. Why? Especially when my children were younger, I could fit online conversations into my personal schedule, like writing email replies after they fell asleep. And for me, written conversations added a level of thoughtfulness, as I'd reread and edit what I was writing for clarity before hitting send.

Back in 2002 when we discovered and chose to begin unschooling, I didn't have any family or friends who had even heard of homeschooling. It was online where I discovered homeschooling, where I found a forum with participants from my province, where I confirmed the legality of keeping my children home instead of sending them to school. Online is where I discovered unschooling, and found a forum where thoughtful and caring parents were discussing the ideas behind it and sharing what it looked like in their family. Unschooling communities are often very small locally, yet rich online where the pool is worldwide. These online connections have made a world of difference for my family.

And over the years I've made many wonderful acquaintances and found my closest friends. Yet I only see them in person once or twice a year—and that's mostly now that my children are older. Are they "real" friends? Definitely. Valuable relationships? Absolutely! What's so fun to observe is that the odd times we do meet face to face, our friendship flows. Conversations pick up from where they left off online, they twist and turn, and after we part ways, they pick up online from that new place. With technological advances, online communication has progressed past written missives to speech and even video. Our communication styles and tools are continually changing, making virtual connections richer.

It's not about valuing one style of communication over another—it's about exploring the styles that work for the communities you and your family find you'd like to be part of. My daughter Lissy first found a community of passionate photographers online, and now, a few years later, she has met quite a few of them in person during her travels, alongside staying in touch with them online. Most of my son Joseph's connections are online, and from them he's learned a lot about developing, managing, and nurturing friendships.

In fact, the conversations I have with each of them surrounding relationships are eerily similar, given that their favoured modes of communication are vastly differ-ent. Our conversations flow through the same topics, the same kinds of questions. That shows me that social inter-actions online are *not* by definition less valuable. I think they range in value just as in person interactions do. Again, the key is to look to your children—support them as they explore the world. Spend as much time helping them navigate online relationships as you would if the other child was visiting in your home.

There are skills that are about being human in our world, like communication and relationship skills, which are sought out and experienced through whatever paths we choose. No matter the window to the world your child chooses, it's the world they can potentially see. Help them explore it, rather than spending your time trying to pull them to your window. Their view may feel uncomfortable to us for a while, but that's *our* learning to do.

Five Unconventional Ideas
about Relationships with Teens

One of the biggest fears I see mentioned over and over by parents is that their teens will make the same mistakes they did growing up. Parents of teens have, at this point in their lives, gained a certain perspective and feel pretty confident about the thread of actions and consequences that wove through their own teen years. Even beyond that, many imagine that if they could go back and do it all again knowing what they know now, they'd do a better job of it. Mired in what they see as the perfect vision of hindsight, their mind starts each flashback with "if only." "If only I'd hung out with a different crowd, I would have made better connections." "If only I hadn't wasted my time, I could have made more money at my job." "If only I had studied harder, I could have gotten into a better college." These are simplistic appraisals, but given what they see as a second chance, parents are confident they can engineer a better outcome for their teen, "if only they would listen to me." (There it is again.)

We could dig deeper and wonder why as adults we are often drawn to tell the negative interpretation of the story of our lives. Maybe it has to do with the pessimistic view of their lives many were handed by their parents? (Though it's helpful to ask ourselves if we really want to hand that tendency to our children.) Why are we drawn to tell people all that is wrong with what we see rather than acknowledge much that is right? Does it make us feel better, smarter? It's fascinating stuff but let's save that rabbit hole for another day. I just wanted to plant that seed. Today let's keep our focus on ways we can support our teens and help them write a different story—their *own* story. Not a shadow of ours.

Back to the rather cynical "if only" recollections. Although I am suggesting that we as parents try to avoid projecting our personal experiences too deeply onto our teens, I don't mean to imply that we keep our thoughts to ourselves and leave our teens to figure out the world on their own. Far from it! Parents have experience and wisdom to share that can be very helpful. Yet to be truly helpful, it's important that our teens receive it in the "no strings attached" spirit we intend, or else our motivation is suspect and the information understandably discounted. So the *atmosphere* of communication is important—the relationship.

Conventionally, relationships with teens are painted as either/or. Either you focus on maintaining authority (tough love) or you avoid challenges altogether (let them run wild). Yet unschooling families have found the beauty of living *inside* the spectrum of those extremes. We continue to cultivate the strong and connected relationships we have built with our children over the years—it's a relationship paradigm that serves us well no matter our children's age. Let's look at some of the ways unschooling parents view relationships differently and what that can look like in the teen years. Notice how all they boil down to how we relate to them: as people, not possessions.

We Drop the Expectations

Unschoolers don't share their experiences or perspective with the expectation that their teens will reach the exact same conclusions. That's hard, isn't it? We know what we know! To us—for us—our experiences are *fact*.

For me, it's a kind of philosophical detachment. Not a detachment as in disengagement, but in appreciation of their individuality. Almost paradoxically, when I'm not living my life through them, I feel even closer to them, because it's not about me—their life is theirs to live—so I can detach from the outcome and drop my expectations. They are not younger versions of me but unique beings in their own right. So though the experiences I share may be helpful to them, useful pieces to the puzzle of their life, I don't expect my stories to mean the same things to them: we are each building different puzzles.

We Realize That the Circumstances of Their Lives Are Different Than Ours

Speaking of different puzzles, take a moment to realize just how different their childhood has been from our own. The pace of change has been accelerating at breakneck speed over our lifetimes. This is a new thing! Comparatively, the pace of change from one generation to the next even just a few decades ago was almost negligible. What an interesting time in human history to be living! But it also means that the passing down of generational experience is more about bigger picture human issues, like empathy and morality, than any day-to-day advice to "do this and get that outcome." The nuts and bolts of our stories are often no longer applicable because the world is changing so rapidly.

For example, even mainstream society is starting to question the typical counsel to "go to college and get a good job at a big company." That was the conventional definition of success in the industrial age, and even deeply into the information age, but we are swiftly moving beyond that now. That advice, so adamantly passed on to us by our parents, has become hopelessly outdated as our teens move into the adulthood.

We Don't Presume We Know Better Than They How They Experience Their Lives

This can be a hard one too. We have more life experience. We remember a time when they were young children and totally dependent on us and we came through for them—here they are! Yet we can also acknowledge that we don't always know what they are thinking and feeling, how they are experiencing and interpreting the day-to-day moments of their lives. Sure, maybe we really enjoyed camping at the lake as a family over the last long weekend, but that doesn't mean they did. And they are not "wrong" to have disliked it. Different personalities and outlooks are just that: different, not wrong.

As I said, none of this is intended to suggest disengagement—that we don't share our experiences, or that we leave them alone to figure out their own lives. What I hope people get out of this discussion is inspiration to listen to teens. They have intelligent information and insights about their own lives to share! Don't discount what they say just because it's different from your thoughts and perspective. Again, it's different, not wrong. Instead, if you try to connect what they're saying with what you already know, you just might create a bigger picture of the world for yourself. *You're learning too.* Which leads to ...

We Don't Assume That as Parents
We're Always Right

This seems to be at the crux of so much parent-teen conflict. At some point, teens are ready for more responsibility, more independence, more freedom. Yet so often parents are determined to keep them in that conventional childhood box as long as possible, the box where parents are right and their children need to do what they're told.

With this new perspective—that their childhood environment is radically different than ours, that they are experiencing life in their own unique ways, and that our expectations are entangled with our life experiences—it is presumptuous of us to believe that our worldview will fit neatly into their lives. What was right for us (or what we imagine would have been right for us), may not be right for them.

Which leads us back to where we started.

Teens Are People Too

Just because they are our children, they are not our possessions. They are people. And just because they are our progeny, doesn't mean we intimately understand them. We need to get to *know* them. And be open so that they get to know us. Build lasting relationships. And from there we have lasting impact on each other's lives. My kids have inspired me countless times! I have learned things from them that have made me a better person. We continue to learn from each other.

From childhood, through the teen years, and beyond, everyone wins with strong, connected, respectful relationships.

CHAPTER SIX

:: family ::

Looking at unschooling from the perspective of the family.

Are You Playing the Role of "Mother"?

Does that seem like a strange question?

Recently I was been remembering life around our house back when it included three children ten and under, with their beautiful yet seemingly endless energy bouncing through the day. I thought about the advice I often hear given to moms of younger children like, "remember to take time for yourself," and I began to ponder the motivation behind those phrases because they never really felt good to me. And it struck me. Phrases like that imply that there are two versions of the one person: the "real" person, "you"; and the "mother".

A quick aside: If you're a dad, I don't mean to specifically exclude you, but these conventional phrases are typically addressed to the mom, so I'm taking that tack here. Feel free to substitute parent and see if you too find yourself wrapped up in a role.

Those meanderings led me to contemplate these questions: Are you not honouring and celebrating yourself *as* you interact with your children? Do you not feel genuinely *you* when you're with them? That you're playing the role of "mother," and not being yourself? Do you think of your time as divided into two distinct slices: "there's time with the kids when I meet their needs and ignore mine" and "time without the kids when I meet my needs and ignore theirs"?

Of course, it's not likely to be quite that black and white, but the questions get our brain juices flowing.

On one hand, putting on that mothering role can feel protective for the mom, like a favourite sweater. It can tell her what to do: "you should play with them," "you should read to them," or "they should take a bath." Yet it can also become judgmental, swirling with echoes of the voices in her head. See what that word "should" does? That level of meta-thinking—thinking about what a "good mother *should* do," while actively mothering—can add a layer between you and your child that gets in the way of deeply connecting with them in the moment. It's like 75 percent of your brain is with them, and the other 25 percent is analyzing and judging every action you take. Instead, try to get fully in the moment *with* them. There is so much joy there.

Of course that doesn't mean don't think about it ever —analyzing our ideas surrounding the parent we want to be and brainstorming ways to get there from where we are now is how we grow as a parent, as a person. But that analysis can get in the way when you're in the moment. Another interesting question: are you doing something with your children because you think you should be doing it or because you know you want to do it? I think pondering that question can help you see the difference between playing a role and being that person.

If you are choosing to be a mother, move beyond playing at it, and *be* it.

For me, this was part of learning to value my work as a mother. Instead of buying into the conventional idea that parenting is second-class work, that I'd be bored with my kids all day if I didn't turn off half my brain and look forward to my time away from my kids to replenish the real me, I decided to bring my full self to each day. I found the many reasons I *choose* to get on the floor and play face to face with my children. To take them to the park. To make messes with them.

That was a big shift for me, realizing I didn't need to be away from my children to be a whole person, to fully be myself. I started looking for things that brought that person out and nurtured her, *while* being with my children. For me, sometimes it was puzzle games with the kids. Or reading a magazine nearby as they played or watched TV. Or reaching for an almost meditative state during repetitive activities like pushing a swing, or separating Lego pieces. A candle lit in the kitchen while I tidied or prepared some food. A light nap as they were engrossed in a movie. A walk around the block giving us all new things to look at, including me checking out the neighbours' front gardens for ideas. A quiet coffee and a book for a half hour before the kids woke up. The whole me is always there.

What do *you* like to do? What refreshes you?

Let's brainstorm some things you might do for a few minutes here and there throughout the day that will help you feel whole and present, not stuck in a role waiting for your moment to step outside it and be yourself:

- dig into what you love: like a few minutes sitting outside with a coffee/tea and a magazine or book—fiction worlds you enjoy or nonfiction about your own interests and passions (while the kids sleep, nap, or run through the sprinkler);
- refresh: like a short midday soak in a bubble bath (while the kids nap or watch TV or join you in the tub);
- get the creative juices flowing: grab a sketchbook or some craft stuff you love and play (with supplies for everyone so kids are welcome to join you, or after they've fallen asleep for the night for more concentrated work);
- change of scenery: a walk or bike ride around the block (alone after dinner while your spouse plays with the kids, or with them during the day, or the whole family);

- get the blood pumping: do some yoga or hooping or trampoline bouncing (again, alone or with the kids—just start and they'll often join in)

Asking yourself these kinds of questions helps bring your focus to *you*. Brainstorm some ideas for yourself and try them out, see how they feel. Obviously you don't have the same time to dedicate to your interests as you did before having children, but that's understandable, right? Children are now one of your passionate interests! And as you do some of these things, even if only for a few minutes here and there, be mindful to give the moment your full attention, truly revel and refresh. Don't have your mind racing about other household stresses while you expertly navigate the stroller around the block. And don't stress if things don't go as planned. Things may not always work out smoothly, but they won't always go awry either. And your children get to see you doing things *you* enjoy. They see you as a whole person, not only as a caregiver.

None of this is to say that you won't find times when the thing you really want to do is to be alone for a while. Or to meet up with a friend. So arrange a trip to the coffee shop or the library while your spouse hangs out with the kids. Seek out an older child as a mother's helper for a while. But from this new perspective, one where you're not looking for an escape but to live fully, you will understand why it's what you need so you're much less likely to feel like you need to justify yourself with phrases like "I'm taking time to honour and celebrate me." Instead you can just say, "I'm going to the coffee shop for some quiet time to write in my journal." You don't need to wait for permission or a special occasion to be yourself.

Drop the role and be yourself—be the mom, and the person, you want to be. At the same time. And bring that whole being into each moment with your children, with your spouse, and with your friends.

Being yourself: it's a refreshing and inspiring place to be.

The Unschooling Family:

Considering Everyone's Needs

When we begin to realize that using our inherent power as adults to control our children interferes with both their learning and our relationships, often our immediate reaction is to pull back. It's a very understandable response, and a great first step.

What can happen though, if parents pull back hard and stay there, is that they often end up ignoring their own needs in favour of their children's. After a while that can lead to feelings of martyrdom, which can lead to expectations that at some point their sacrifice will be acknowledged, and possibly bitterness when that doesn't happen. "I give and give and I don't think I can give any more." Burn out.

Or, for parents still caught up in the notion of "us and them" but trying to maintain a sense of balance, life can get overwhelming. Balancing power is like trying to balance a teeter-totter: it's just damn hard. Why? Because when power is a factor, it can lead to decisions that seem random and inexplicable. Decisions become focused around an arbitrary fulcrum point, instead of on everyone's needs. "Why did you let me do that last week, and not this week?" "Well, last week you got do all sorts of things you wanted to do, so this week I'd like to choose some stuff." When decisions are based on someone's arbitrary view of "balance," the people involved can feel wronged and discussions can go on and on without resolution. There is almost always a "but" to be added. Parenting becomes more intense and challenging than it needs to be. Burn out.

What's my point? Dropping the "us and them" paradigm not only better supports unschooling and long-term family relationships, it also makes parenting a less contentious and more rewarding endeavour. But at the same time, it's important that parents express their needs too. It's important that everyone's needs are considered.

It's pretty easy to say but not so easy to do. It takes experience. It takes understanding each other's needs and personalities. It takes trust. And all those things take time to develop. But keep trying. Everyone in the family will get better at it over time.

It can feel a bit scary at first, bringing our needs into the discussion. Maybe this is something new to you because as a kid (or adult!) you were never asked to verbalize them. Maybe you're worried you're asking for too much. Maybe you've heard the reminder to "say yes" more and you're worried you're not being supportive enough of your kids' needs. But don't wait until you think you have yourself all figured out before saying something—nobody is perfect at this. But that's the great thing about doing it as a family: you'll get feedback. You'll give feedback. You're all working together.

What kind of internal work can we as parents do to help the process along? Take the time to ensure we bring real needs to the table. Not whims, or wishes, or whatevers, but real needs. If you're quite sure the request in front of you needs a "not right now" answer because you really need to eat something immediately or else your frustration will spill over, do it. Explain that. And go eat something right now. And see how that works out. Remember, a "no" in this moment doesn't mean that every time for the foreseeable future that you feel hungry you need to say no. And if you say you need to do something right now and then you don't end up doing it right now, that's a clue to reconsider next time.

Examine and evaluate your needs. Evaluate if fulfilling them helped. Tweak them. That examination also helps ensure that power does not sneak into the equation—watch out for self-talk like "I'm the adult; I should be able to do XX." This process is where you'll find those leftover unexamined beliefs you were handed. Watch out for words like "should" and "have to." Maybe they are true for you, maybe they aren't. But until you examine them, you won't know. And as a bonus, once you examine them, you can explain them to others if you decide they are a real need of yours, at least in this moment. That builds trust.

It's interesting to note that kids usually have much less work to do in this department because they haven't had a childhood full of "you can do that when you're an adult" situations handed to them. They are already pretty good at expressing what they are sincerely interested in doing.

Beyond burn out, what else can happen if parents ignore their own needs? I think we're doing our kids a disservice if we don't show them that others may have differing perspectives or needs; that it's worthwhile to take the time to consider the needs of others involved in a situation and find an inclusive path forward. And that path can look different each time, even with the same people. This effort helps build strong and trusting relationships. And it's a wonderful skill to develop. In fact, from conversations with my children as young adults, this seems to be one of the more prevalent social skills that's lacking as they meet more and more people out and about in the world: many people seem to have a hard time anticipating the impact their choices might have on those around them.

What else? If a parent chooses not to express their needs, their children may interpret those actions as "the way to make the people I love happy is to ignore my needs and satisfy theirs" and bring that attitude to their future relationships. That might not work out very well for them.

But adding our needs doesn't mean we have to be dogmatic about it. We can express our needs and choose to gift our kids with extra attention, extra supplies, extra anything. Expressing our needs helps them understand when we're going above and beyond so it doesn't become an expectation.

Not just "yes", but "I'm tired, but I know how much you'd like me to watch that show with you. I'll do my best to stay awake!"

Not just "yes", but "I bet you'll have so much fun with that toy! I'll help you pay for it out of my fun money."

Not only are kids learning to trust that their parents will help them meet their needs, parents are learning to trust their kids too. Trust that their kids will only ask for what they really feel they need. This allows parents to be more comfortable stretching themselves, going above and beyond to meet their kids' real needs, trusting that there will be time to satisfy their own needs as well.

And you'll get better at it with experience. You'll get better at understanding the motivations behind their requests to do things, helping you feel more motivated to support them. You'll get better at understanding your own real limitations, helping you take better care of yourself, and to push through when you're more restless than tired. You'll have a better grasp on which tools help both you and your kids move more smoothly through frustration.

Over time, you will all get to know each other better, your relationships will get stronger and the trust between you will grow. All those things will help make the "figuring out a path forward" moments go more smoothly.

The great thing about envisioning your family as a wonderful team with the power of everyone in the family behind it is that it actually helps remind you to bring your needs to the table: you're part of the team. It helps us remember to consider everyone's needs. And that helps us develop the strong relationships and trust with our children that are the foundation of a thriving unschooling home.

Life with Children

Unschooling with children is an incredibly busy and exciting time. They often bounce up in the morning and dash straight to their activity of choice, their boundless energy propelling them through the day, from activity to activity, until they drop with exhaustion. I remember wishing many times that I had their energy! Some evenings I walked through the house, tallying the bursts of imagination and play that had consumed them that day: a tableau of stuffed animals on the couch; a marble maze built in the corner of the play room; a Pokémon battle scene depicted on the kitchen table; swirls of shaving cream drying out on the bathtub walls; video game controllers askew in front of the TV; the dress-up box empty and toy swords and crowns strewn around, the detritus of battle.

Winding down at night, maybe watching a movie or playing a video game, I might start to tidy up. Sometimes they'd help out—more often if I remembered to suggest a small and specific task, "Can you toss the stuffed animals in the bin?" Sometimes I'd tidy up after they fell asleep, surprising them with a fresh canvas when they came down the next morning. Sometimes the house was just as they left it, and seeing the stuffed animals frozen mid-scene inspiring them to pick up their game where they left off. Every day is a new day of fun and exploration for them, even when as parents we sometimes lose track of what day of the week it happens to be.

So just what are they up to?

Exploring and Learning about the World

Childhood play and learning is fascinating. As they reach out into the world so much is new to them! Pirate movies. Bike riding. Pioneer villages. Building toys. Science centres. Water play. Somersaults. Museums with dinosaurs. Fantastical stories with dragons and magic. Baking cookies. Piles of leaves. Board games. Video games. Card games. Dice games. Hide and seek. The questions fly: Why are you doing that? How do you do that? Why does that happen? How does that work? At times you may feel like a walking reference library; other times you seriously consider investing money in your best friend Google. Through their play, children process and explore and connect all the new facts and ideas they encounter, learning all the while.

How can you support them? Let their minds roam free—that's where the best learning is because that's what their mind is thirsty for in the moment. Be their companion in play when asked (or offered and accepted) to support and expand their exploration. Answer their questions earnestly, or look them up, so they never stop asking. Share their excitement and wonder to stay deeply connected with them. Offer up food and drink regularly to keep them fueled. Share what you know beforehand about the places you go so they begin to understand the world around them. Be patient. And when you're tired, sit and watch them for a while. Children are pretty awe-inspiring beings.

Exploring and Learning about Themselves

As well as all that learning about the world, they are also learning so much about themselves. Their reactions are often visceral—immediate and strong: deep sadness and frustration when things don't go as envisioned; bursting joy when they do; overflowing anticipation for upcoming events; overwhelming fear of things that scare them. As you are their reliable extra set of hands as they explore the physical world, you're also their solid anchor as they navigate their emotional world.

How can you support them? Meet them where they are, emotionally and physically—kneel down to meet them eye to eye, or sweep them up in your arms. See the situation through their eyes. Share their excitement or empathize with their challenges. Listen to them, talk with them—either in the moment, or later when things settle, or both. Figure out how you can best help *them* process their emotions by looking to your child for clues. And don't assume the process will be the same for all your children. If they're receptive, point out things you notice that you think might help them make a connection: "It can be hard to concentrate when you're tired."

Be their anchor, their safe place, and build a strong relationship with them. Trust and learning will blossom.

Living Together

A child's curiosity and enthusiasm for life is contagious—if you let it wash over you instead of trying to tamp it down. Looking back, those moments when I remembered to be amazed at their persistence instead of battling it would often re-energize me. I eventually discovered a pattern: the exhausting days were those when I tried to make them fit *my* schedule. I asked myself what I was trying to accomplish with that. They often enjoyed the comfort of routine—knowing generally how the day flowed, how we'd get ready to go out, and so on but a routine is not time dependent like a schedule. So I stopped watching the clock and instead watched them. They were so beautifully curious, and much happier, when they followed their needs and interests, from the earliest ages. And I noticed that I was happier too when I wasn't continually trying to redirect them; trying to coax them to adhere to my vision of what our lives "should" look like. More deschooling.

Without my shepherding, most of our days, weeks, months had a wonderful flow to them, with everyone's needs rippling through. And what I discovered is that their free lives were, and continue to be, so much more interesting I could *ever* have envisioned! Take some time to remember the ways your family's lives sweetly flow together when there isn't outside pressure being brought to bear on the day. And try to create more of that.

What's behind a Typical Unschooling Day?

It's kind of funny to think in terms of "typical" when talking about what unschooling days look like. I mean, one of the things I often emphasize is how different unschooling in action can look from family to family, even from child to child. Yet there is a basic motif that underscores our actions with our children, even when those actions vary widely.

Being Available, Willing, and Supportive

Being available to talk, willing to help, and supportive of their goals. Not just with words, but with our actions.

Here's a little story. In 2012 when I decided I wanted to write on my blog more consistently and I was working on *Free to Live*, I thought it would be helpful to set up a writing area out of the way to minimize distractions so I set up a desk in the basement. It was a nice area: under a window, lots of wall space to tack up my notes, power for my laptop and a desk lamp. I had fun setting it up!

I think I lasted about a week and a half. I felt too out of the loop, too unavailable. I wasn't nearby for a quick chat or a question, or to notice if something was starting to go off the rails and tweak something to help our day flow more smoothly. So I moved back up to the library, smack dab in the middle of the house—the hub whose spokes lead to the kitchen, the bedrooms, the family room and more. Okay, I just counted how many doorways lead out of this seemingly small room: six. It *is* the crossroads of our home!

This is where I feel comfortable writing. I sometimes use headphones to keep random and distracting sounds at bay. Everyone that passes by can see I'm writing, or working away at something. Yet they know if they need me for anything I am happy to stop and help them out (and I mean it—I am mindful not to carelessly react with frustration at an interruption). I peripherally notice the comings and goings: snacks being grabbed, someone going outside for a walk, another going downstairs for something. I can sense frustration through body language and check in to see what's up. I am available and willing to help.

Not surprisingly, when my kids were younger being available and willing to help looked a lot different! That's a much more physical phase of parenting, yet very important for their emotional development: when you support their physical needs, from food to sleep to play, you are building the loving and supportive foundation from which their lives will branch out. Playing board games and video games and watching Blue's Clues and drawing clues and reading stories and grabbing drinks and helping work through frustrations and disagreements: your children aren't yet able to do many things and you are their more experienced hands. Just remember, this isn't a time to push beyond your limits—be honest with yourself and your family. It's also a wonderful time to explore those limits, to discover what you are capable of.

Nowadays it's driving places and text chats and sharing interesting information and earnest conversations and trying new recipes and organizing activities and looking up US tax info and reorganizing rooms and "good morning!" and clinic visits and snow shoveling and Mario Party 9. Seeing the world through their eyes gives meaning and purpose to every one of these activities. Supporting our children as they explore the world, at every age, is a great way for *all* of us to learn.

And as unschooling goes, your days may look very different from my days. Not only will our family's interests and personalities differ, our circumstances are surely different as well. Maybe you work part-time outside the home, or are a single parent working from home, or you and your spouse both work from home, or you live in a multi-family home, or your children spend some time being cared for by others. The possibilities for what your particular unschooling days look like are vast, but the motif stays the same: being available, willing, and supportive. Having some fixed parameters in your lives like work hours or one car to share or whatever realities are part of your landscape doesn't mean unschooling can't flourish. It means what it has meant for all of us: working together as a family to find ways to support each other's needs and dreams; being creative and open to unconventional ideas.

Is it working? The key is to look to your children. Do *they* feel that you are available for them? That you are willing to help them reach their goals? That you are supportive of their interests and activities? Are they happy? Let those answers guide you to create and maintain a supportive unschooling atmosphere that values them as individuals and supports their learning, no matter your circumstances. It's not about trying to ignore reality and pretend our lives are "perfect," but about living our real lives; our typical days.

Enjoying Visits with Extended Family

Many of us are the lone unschooling family when our families of origin gather for holiday celebrations, birthdays, reunions and so on. That is certainly true in our case, both for visiting with my own family and my spouse's. The choices we're making as parents are very different than those of many others, and sometimes we can feel a bit isolated even in a crowded room. So I thought I'd share a few things I do to set these visits up for success.

First, things go much more smoothly for me when I remember that I'm choosing to visit, or to invite others over. I don't "have to" see anyone. I won't be arrested or jailed for not visiting with my relatives. So right off, it's my choice. It's a much better mindset because from that perspective I see opportunity, not obligation. And if I'm choosing to go and hoping to avoid friction, then it's worth the time and effort for me to set up the visit to be successful.

Answering Questions

Because we are doing things differently, we are interesting—or at least a curiosity—so chances are our relatives will ask questions. It's so easy to feel defensive when others ask about how we are raising our children; it's deeply personal. And maybe the questions are meant confrontationally, maybe not. But it works best for me not to get pulled into that quagmire. That's part of the work I choose to do, to shift past any defensiveness before answering and assume there is honest interest somewhere behind the question.

You may cringe at hearing some version of the same old question, maybe "Are you guys still homeschooling?" Or unschooling. Or whatever words you've used in conversation to describe what you're doing. Even if you feel what they really mean is "have you come to your senses yet?" you don't have to react with some version of "yes, we are and we will be doing this forever so get used to it."

There's no need to draw a line in the sand over personal parenting and educational choices. That can invite argument because it can feel to others that you're implicitly judging their choices. "It's working well for us now" is a fine answer that is both truthful and open to the understanding that people and circumstances can change. And without that tone of finality it can, without any direct words at all, help other parents realize that they too can change their minds; if their kids are in school, it might be working well for them now, but people and circumstances can change.

One thing I don't do in conversation though is invite their opinion about what we're doing. I love them, but I am choosing to create a different parenting paradigm than their worldview so what kinds of answers would I expect to get? It's a family gathering, not a parenting conference. I remind myself not to have any expectation of, or need for, their support. If I have questions, or want in-depth conversation about parenting or learning or education, I wait until I'm in a group of unschoolers, face to face or online, because that's the filter through which I am looking for answers.

I also don't grouse about my kids, or any parenting challenges in general, because that's just a question in disguise: family members want to be helpful and will likely volunteer any solutions they see. But again, they'd be coming from a different perspective than what I'm looking for so that experience would just be frustrating for both of us. Not my goal.

And remember, if any conversation starts to feel uncomfortable, feel free to change the subject, or go to the bathroom, or go play with the kids, or take the kids for a walk around the block, or pull out a game and invite others, adults and kids, to play. You aren't a hostage even if you're in someone else's home.

Conversation Starters and Activities on Hand

Questions are great conversation starters and subject changers. But, as I mentioned above, steer clear of topics where you already know your opinions differ. I wouldn't walk up to my sister-in-law the retired teacher and say "Did you see that article online about how homework sucks?" Others can feel attacked just as easily as we can.

Instead, I love to ask questions about their interests, maybe because curiously, many conventional adults I talk to don't seem to think they have any. I like inviting them to think about themselves. It's also a great conversation starter with kids because, if interested in chatting, they can talk and talk about their passions. Or they might invite me to play or watch or whatever. I love seeing their eyes light up! And I get to learn more about them.

And not to be subversive or anything, but you're also introducing them to the world of passions and interests and how fun it can be to immerse yourself in something, not to mention discovering how much you learn along the way: the basis for unschooling. If you can draw them in through doing, maybe one day they might begin to understand where you're coming from. Or not—you're just planting a seed.

Also, before you go, take the time to think about who's going to be there and what they like. It helps you have interesting questions at the ready. You can talk to your kids before you go too. "Hey, remember Grammy showed us that sweater she was knitting last time we saw her, let's remember to ask her if she's finished yet." Or "Aunt Sue loves to be outside, why don't we invite her to walk to the park down the road?" Or "We'll probably eat lunch when we get there, but after do you guys want to ask Grandpa to play Crazy Eights? It's his favourite card game." Or even the other way sometimes. I've called my

Mom before we visit, "Hey Mom, the kids are really into Monopoly in this week, if I bring the game do you want to play with us?" If she does, great; if she doesn't, I can let the kids know ahead of time and we can come up with something else to bring or do during our visit.

Giving everyone a heads up lets them look forward to things, brings to mind things they both enjoy so conversation starts more easily, and even gives them a head start in coming up with a response instead of feeling put on the spot. "I don't really like Crazy Eights, can we play War? I'll show you how to play, Grandpa!"

I'd also keep a peripheral eye on what was up with my kids. If I noticed a relative starting a conversation, I'd watch to make sure my kids were comfortable. If not, I wouldn't leave them to struggle or be quizzed, I'd join them. Maybe for moral support, maybe answering questions for them, maybe changing the topic, or maybe inviting them to join me somewhere else. My actions were dependent on any plans we'd made beforehand, during our informal briefing, and whatever I saw happening in the moment itself.

Another thing I did when we went to visit relatives was bring toys, games, and/or crafts for my kids, things they would like to play with so they weren't bored. The point was for them to enjoy the visit too! Depending on who we were visiting, I'd also bring things we could all do together—children and adults. From something as simple as card games like Go Fish, to Bingo, to Monopoly, we've enjoyed many games over the years. If the adults are amenable, games can be a great way to spend time together where kids can be kids, the adults can get to know them better, and the pressure of conversation is minimal. And time passes much more joyfully when you're having fun!

Have a Plan

If things have a habit of going off the rails once the "things" are done and conversations are left to meander and flow and potentially get away from people, understand that and plan for it ahead of time. For example, maybe plan to leave after dinner is done. And say it firmly when you arrive (if you're asked) so you don't invite someone to try to coerce or guilt you into staying longer.

And especially when the kids are younger, spend lots of time with the kids. They are learning about navigating relatives too! They need and appreciate your attention and company. The typical "adults in one room, kids in the other" did not seem to work very well. I was often the lone adult hanging with the kids, playing games, having fun, and enjoying wonderful and sincere conversations. And it meant there weren't kid battles for the adults to complain or yell about. And bonus, they weren't complaining about my kids!

A little time and planning before any visit with extended family can go a long way to helping it play out with less frustration and lots more fun. Enjoy!

Supporting Our Kids' Relationships
with Their Relatives

With unschooling we talk quite a bit about not having expectations of our children because that adds a filter to the relationship that gets in the way of both learning and living. It's much more helpful to look clearly at our children as they are today. I'd extend that to any relationship and encourage dropping expectations of your extended family as well. Get to know the real person, not the role. Work with that. Don't try to change them into your dream grandparent or aunt or uncle to your child. Remember, this is their journey too. They are discovering the kind of grandparent or aunt or uncle they want to be. You can help that journey along. Not by trying to mold them into your vision of that relationship, but by helping them experience and explore their vision.

Same with your children: support them as they create their own relationships with their relatives. At family gatherings, try to look at interactions from your child's perspective. It's not about how I feel about the conversation; it's about how my child feels about it. (I'm assuming you don't think the relative is subversively manipulating your child; and if you do, I'd probably ask why you were there in the first place.) Each time I can shift and see my children's lives from their perspective it leads to better actions and reactions on my part—better meaning more supportive of them. From that perspective, not only do I

feel less pressure to control things, I'm also excited to discover what kind of relationship develops.

And I'm a really great resource to help them with
that! I know my parents, my siblings, and my extended
family pretty well from many years of experience; like-
wise, my spouse knows his family well. And obviously I
know my kids better than they do. So I can take some time
to figure out how I might best nurture a developing relationship between them. That doesn't mean trying to get
one of them to compromise or change for the other (that's
a clue that I've taken over responsibility for the relationship); it's about searching out their common ground.

How might I do that? By asking myself all sorts of
questions. Would my Mom (insert any relative in question) enjoy hands-on play with my children? Does she feel
like she's connecting with them when they are excitedly
playing with and showing her their favourite toys? Then
bring them. Or does that level of energy and activity feel
overwhelming to her, and she'd feel more relaxed and
connected playing board or cards games or reading their
favourite picture books with them. Bring those. Or might
she prefer sitting more quietly and enjoying a favourite
movie? Suggest your kids choose a few of their favourite
movies or shows to bring and ask Grammy to pick which
one she'd like to watch with them. And then initiate these
activities at an appropriate time during the visit.

If your parents are more hands-off and mostly want
to see their grandchildren but not particularly interact
with them, bring things your kids will enjoy doing to pass
the time. Your parents will see their grandkids: happy par-

ents. Your kids will have fun stuff to keep them busy: happy kids. Remember, this might be how it looks now, but that doesn't mean it'll be that way forever. A hands-off grandparent may, after a while, realize they don't know their grandchild very well and start interacting more. That realization may take longer to come to if they have to work through feelings of being judged by you as well. If you can keep the relationship as clear of judgment as possible, it allows them to evaluate and learn and grow more directly.

If your child is looking for more interaction, be the example. Say your child brings their favourite toy with them to show their aunt. You can watch out for that moment and join them, being the facilitator. Explain your child's excitement to your sister. You could smile and say "He can play with his transformers for hours, figuring out exactly how all the bits fit together as they move from one thing into another." And then to your child, "Oh! I bet she'd like to see your blue transformer, how you can get it from car to robot in five seconds." Maybe make a game of counting out how long it takes to transform it back and forth a couple times. You're acknowledging your child's excitement and showing your sister how she might interact. Plus, you're pointing out the particular things your child enjoys about the toy/activity so that she gets to know him a little bit better.

But still, you needn't expect that she get any better at the relationship—at this point you're more supporting your child's wish to share their joy with their aunt. Maybe your sister gets to know your child better and begins to enjoy when they shares their interests, taking over the conversations so you no longer need to facilitate. Or maybe as your child gets older they come to realize that their aunt simply doesn't want to know much detail about their interests. You can commiserate with them and move on to other things.

These aren't meant as definitive actions, but more to help get your juices flowing to discover ways *your* relatives and children might enjoy interacting. Don't be frustrated if your initial ideas don't work out well; keep trying. And remember, we're looking for common ground, supportive ways to bring the perspectives of both the child and the relative in question together. Take the time to see things through both their points of view and you will be in the best position to nurture the development of a lifelong relationship that meets both their desires as much as possible.

But if one is wishing for more of a relationship than the other is interested in, that is just the way it is for now. Just as you can't force them to fit into your vision of that relationship, neither can one of them force the other to submit to their vision without further damaging the relationship. Once your conversations with them have revealed an impasse in that moment, conversations with the one feeling slighted can swirl around people and personalities and wishes and that this moment doesn't define forever. People grow and change. It's a beautiful dance. It's life.

When Negative Relatives Won't Let Go

I thought it might be helpful to dig a bit more into ways you can deal with relatives who are more insistent about their negative viewpoint about your lifestyle. Maybe when you change the subject, they look for any opening to change it back; maybe when you leave the conversation to go somewhere else they soon seek you out and start it back up; maybe they continue to express deep concern that your choices are ruining your children.

Before your next visit, it can help to take some time to think about their childhood, their parents, their educational experiences, their life experiences, and see how that thread led them to the confident stance they are taking with you today. Their journey is definitely different from yours! Imagine all the beliefs about parenting and learning they have to question in themselves to even begin to understand the advantages and possibilities of your unschooling lifestyle.

That's a lot to ask of them—they just may not be willing to do it right now. At this point, a heated exchange of facts and beliefs isn't likely to change anyone's mind, just escalate the frustration and stress. It can help to remember that they are probably acting out of concern and love for their grandchild, or niece or nephew, yet you and your family shouldn't suffer as a result of your differing viewpoints. When negative relatives get stuck on trying to change you rather than trying to understand your choices, and you are uncomfortable with their attitude and questions, I would suggest that you show them you understand their concerns and then actively disengage. Maybe something like, "I think it's great that you care about my kids so much, however, how we raise them is our choice and responsibility. This is working well for us right now and it's not up for discussion."

If possible, it's probably better at that point to change the topic of discussion to a neutral subject rather than walk away. Walking away can imply that the entire relationship rests on resolving the disagreement over your educational choices/lifestyle, while changing the topic leaves the impression that, though that particular topic is off-limits for now, you aren't dismissing them as a person because of your differing points of view. So ... fishing? Home decorating? Movies? How are things at work? And if they choose to leave the conversation in a huff, hey, that's their choice too. You've planted the seed that this disagreement isn't the end of the world and have tried to make it about the ideas, not the people. If they come back to the conversation you can just remind them, "Hey, we weren't going to talk about that any more, remember?" And change the subject. Again.

If you think they would be amenable to learning more about unschooling but are, for some reason or other, discounting the information they get from you, you could loan them a book about unschooling. Or send them a couple links to websites you've found helpful. It puts a bit of a cushion between you, and pulls the focus away from the people and onto the ideas. Or even better, of those resources you've found helpful, pick a couple that you think might meet them where they are in their understanding and that will, from there, walk them through the principles and ideas behind unschooling. But don't overwhelm them with too much information or they may not even start.

And you can leave them an opening: "I'd be happy to answer any questions you have after you've read some of this information." Next time they bring up the topic ask if they've read the information you sent along, and if not, say you don't want to rehash the same old conversation. Change the topic. If they have, you could say "That's cool, do you have questions from that?" If you discover they really only read it defensively to pick out points to argue, you know they aren't yet open to learning about unschooling. Good to know. Change the topic.

I know I keep saying change the topic, but really, it's that simple. Or politely leave the conversation entirely. A conversation takes two people and if you don't see any positive reason to engage, don't. For now, just practice that. Maybe you wish your relationships with extended family were deeper, but it's not something you can force. You don't need them to understand your choices right now. Remember that while they may be determined to tell you why your educational and parenting choices are wrong, those aren't the only subjects in the world. Find others. And over time, without the pressure to come to agreement, even your negative relatives will see your children blossom with unschooling; they will see the beautiful relationships you have with your children in action. Show them, don't tell them—that works all over the place, doesn't it? Be patient.

Meanwhile, focus on the fun and interesting ways you can connect with them. Light conversations, games, playing outside, a polite hello and good bye, etc. You can try to keep the relationships cordial until the kids are old enough that child-rearing fades away as a topic altogether. At that point your relatives will likely begin to develop real relationships with your children, based on shared interests and connections. And that's where you wanted to be all along.

:: lifestyle ::

Musings on unschooling as a lifestyle.

Why Choice is Key in
Learning Life Skills

The unschooling lifestyle in support of learning life skills is a wonderful dance of everyday living, relationships, and choice:

- The usefulness of these life skills shows up in the *everyday living*—eating, sleeping, taking care of our bodies, taking care of our stuff, maintaining our environment, etc.

- We live with others in both our family and our extended community, so *relationships* weave through everything.

- And unschooling learning itself, academic or otherwise, boils down to *choice*. That is where the best learning is because that's where the person's thoughts are swirling, where their thinking is leading them: to make this particular choice. They know the motivation behind their choice and are interested in seeing how it plays out, whether it's to mix the baking soda and vinegar, to use a particular strategy for a boss battle, or to stay awake to watch the rest of the movie.

This learning through the exploration of their environment is not so much about the individual choices themselves but about the process: our children experience the results and then incorporate them into their understanding of themselves and the world. And from that place of deeper understanding they make their next choice. And they gain more experience. And then they make their next choice, and so on. That's the process of real learning—learning that is understood and remembered because it is meaningful to them.

Yet as parents, it's easy to get caught up in the moment of each decision because often we envision that the choice they're wanting to make now, "if we let them," is the choice they'll make again and again and again into adulthood. Our fear extrapolates this moment far into the future: "If I let them stay up late and sleep in, they'll never be able to get up for a job."; "If I let them eat ice cream for breakfast, they'll never want to eat eggs for breakfast again."; or "If I let them choose whether to help out around the house, they'll never help."

The choices our children make today as they explore the world *aren't* cast in stone moving forward. In fact, one of the interesting things they learn through making choices is that making different choices in the future doesn't mean they were "wrong" before—maybe they have different goals now, or can see more options, or can better predict an outcome. Through this process they gain experience that helps them get better at both analyzing situations and making choices that more often work out as anticipated. They also see how their preferences and goals change over time, and how their choices change accordingly; meaning they learn a lot more about how they work too. So much more learning than just following a rule.

Another interesting shift happens when our children know they are free to make their own choices. Their perspective moves from feeling like they are "getting away with something," to honestly evaluating their environment, the circumstances in the moment, their goals, their options, and then making what they believe is their best choice in the moment. They take ownership and responsibility for their actions. Yet giving children the opportunity to make choices doesn't mean that the parents are out of the picture—our role is just different. Instead of stating a rule, unschooling parents share their experience and perspective, adding it to the mix of information being considered.

Two areas of life skills often questioned as people are learning about unschooling are sleep and food but they boil down to the same idea: exploring living through choices. Some imagine chaos, yet our children don't explore in a vacuum—they live with their family and real limitations. There is a family budget for food. There are other people in the family that also want to eat—and sleep. There will be appointments to be kept and activities at certain times that they'll want to get to. Reality. The big shift for parents is, instead of thinking in terms of limits which shut down exploration and learning, to think in terms of figuring out ways for everyone to meet their needs and goals: *help* them explore.

As an example, one reason I hear pretty regularly for set bedtimes isn't related to the children's sleep itself, but to the at-home parent looking for a break in the evening. And that's understandable. Yet a bedtime for the kids isn't the only possible solution to meet that need. If the children are looking to stay up later and the at-home parent is looking for some quiet time, brainstorm some ideas to try to meet *both* those needs. Ask the kids for ideas too—that helps them begin to see the scope of considerations beyond themselves.

Maybe the spouse/partner can plan some focused board game time or story time with the kids while the other parent has some quiet time to read or take a walk or whatever they find relaxing and centring. And does it actually need to be in the evening? Maybe they'd enjoy getting up earlier in the morning to have some solitude and space for their projects. Or maybe the at-home parent discovers a rejuvenating activity they can do during the day and the children happily choose to join in—or decide to keep themselves otherwise occupied. Those are just a few ideas but I imagine you get the picture. Try something and if that doesn't work out try something else.

I know it's easy to say—"keep trying different things and see how they work out"—but not so easy to do. It *is* challenging to work things out with real people seemingly at cross-purposes. It does take a lot of time to talk with those involved, to do the work to understand our own needs and explain them, to see things from the perspectives of others and empathize with their needs, to brainstorm possible solutions, to try them out and see how things go, and to tweak it by doing the whole process all over again and again. And what works now may not work six months from now—people, children and adults, change.

But in my experience it's definitely worth the effort, both in terms of the incredible amount of learning about living everyone is doing *and* in terms of the depth of your relationships. The connected and trusting relationships developed over the years are priceless.

Unschooling with Strong Beliefs

In case you haven't yet come across the idea of rules versus principles as related to unschooling, here's a super quick summary. Rules are often used as shortcuts—substitutes for thinking in the moment. "In that situation, always do this." What to do. On the other hand, principles encourage the discussion and evaluation of a situation. *Why* you'd choose to do it. Working with principles means more experience analyzing circumstances. More experience seeing situations from others' perspectives. More experience brainstorming possible paths forward.

Living by principles to guide choices sounds pretty logical when real learning—learning that is understood and remembered—is the goal. And not only are the discussions an opportunity to understand each other a bit better, the process minimizes power struggles between adults and children because the conversations aren't fraught with "do as you're told" edicts. The downside? It takes time. But without the stress of rushing the kids through a day dictated by a school schedule and evening homework, you have the time to help them develop this valuable skill.

But what if there is an area of life that you've already spent a lot of time analyzing and have come to some pretty solid conclusions? What if you have some pretty strong beliefs? These beliefs are truths for you. Your life feels better living this way and you believe your child would be better off living this way too.

It *is* hard to imagine that your child may not hold the same beliefs as you. That they may not draw the same conclusions as you do from the same set of facts. Yet it's true. Your child is not a carbon copy of you—they are a beautifully unique combination of genetic material wired to think their own thoughts.

Certainly when they are younger you have much greater control over their environment, over what comes into your home. You just don't cook or serve meat. Or you don't buy processed foods and you do your own baking. Or you go to a place of worship every week. Or you faithfully recycle and bike most places. Or you don't have a TV. It's just what your family does.

The turning point comes when your child becomes aware that other options exist. In that moment, you may feel a rising fear of dissent, a fear mired in all those reasons you chose to eschew those options in the first place. Maybe your fear pushes you to let your strong principles become rigid rules. Yet fear is not a good motivator for making choices. And rules aren't a good tool for real learning.

What else might you do? You can choose to share with your children information about why you do the things you do. In digestible chunks as it comes up—not in a big, sit-down, "I'm going to convince you why I'm right" talks. Remember, your strong beliefs developed *after* you were interested enough to dive deeply into the topic, learning and questioning and developing your own understanding. In moments *when they are interested*, share a bit more information. Not just stuff edited for your view. The surrounding bits too. Real learning.

Let's play with an example. Maybe you're staunchly vegetarian. You have your reasons: maybe they're mostly health based; maybe they're based on your thoughts surrounding animal cruelty; maybe you find the texture of meat in general unappealing. Whatever your reason, that's great!

Yet when your child discovers that some people eat meat, how will you react to their curiosity? Maybe you share briefly why you guys don't eat it, in language that is appropriate for your child (remember, don't try to create fear). Maybe that satisfies their curiosity for now. Maybe they ask some more questions and you continue the conversation until they move on.

But supporting their exploration doesn't mean you need to toss your principles out the window. Take the time to understand your thoughts surrounding the situation. That's important, not only so that you don't feel unduly pressured to act contrary to your principles, but also so that you can share your thoughts to help them understand how you came to your conclusion.

Then maybe at some point they're interested in trying some meat. Let's brainstorm a few ways things might go:

- Maybe you are comfortable picking up some meat at the store, or the farm, next time you're out and cooking it up, while not eating it yourself. Ask what they might like to try and chat about that.

- Maybe you're not comfortable buying and/or cooking it, but you're comfortable with someone else doing it. Maybe your spouse? Maybe your child is old enough to do it? If the smell would bother you, you could go out for a couple hours.

- If that would bother you, maybe you arrange for your child to visit family or friends for a meat-based meal. Or ask someone to take them to a restaurant to try it.

There are *many* ways to respect your principles while still supporting your child's wish to explore.

And if in the end you choose to place your principles above your child's exploration and learning, do so mindfully—understand the potential ramifications. From your child's perspective, there's a good chance they will, at some point, be drawn to exploring the topic. In fact, by drawing a line in the sand, chances are your child will probably be pretty curious about what's on the other side. But with your firm stance, they'll also know they need to do it under your radar. If that happens, you obviously won't be there to talk with them, nor will they likely feel comfortable coming to you to talk about it after. That may or may not be a biggie. They may or may not resent the fact that you have forbidden a piece of the world. It may put a strain your relationship. They may trust you a bit less. Make the choice mindfully.

And if you choose that path, I'd suggest you try not to react judgmentally if you discover they have been exploring "behind your back." Remember, your choice set up that paradigm. "You had burgers over at Tom's house? Did you like them? What did you put on it?" Even if you couldn't in good conscience have arranged the meal over at Tom's place, it will do nothing but hurt your relationship to condemn your child for trying the meat (or the cookie, or the TV show) when they were curious and had the opportunity.

And heads up, you might also find yourself in the reverse situation—I know I have! As your children get older, they may hold, or choose to explore, strong beliefs that you don't personally hold. Maybe *they* choose to eat vegetarian, or vegan, or want to explore a religion. Do you still support them? I hope so. Is your support lukewarm? I hope not. The world is full of fascinating opportunities and supporting their exploration and learning is golden. You may find that you and your children don't hold all the same beliefs and principles, but you do share the passion and self-awareness that drives them. Celebrate that.

Chores For Cash—A Fair Exchange?

Money is still a rather taboo subject, even in families. But it's another area of life skills that everyone can learn more about by digging in instead. I spent time doing my own work—asking myself "why" and "what if" questions, exploring my fear and reluctance, understanding my own goals—so that I could feel comfortable being open about money with my children. I still do as I discover new pockets of old thoughts.

So how might we explore money with them?

When the kids are young, play games together that involve money. Many video games have a currency component, and there are classic board games, like Monopoly and Life, and their digital counterparts. When they're interested, help them open up a bank account. Log into it online with them, regularly. After they use their bank card, log in again. As they get older, balance your bank account and pay your bills when they're around. Chat about the family budget. Ask for their input on what the next home improvement project might be. Over the years so many money-related topics nudge our lives.

Beyond understanding how money flows through our lives, understanding our personal spending habits is also a great life skill to develop. To help my children explore the area of money management, it made a lot of sense to me to give them some money to manage. For us, that was usually through an allowance.

Some parents are tempted to tie their children's allowance to chores, likening it to work and salary, and using it as a tool of coercion, "If you don't finish your chores by Sunday night you won't be getting your allowance this week." But for us the main purpose wasn't to convince our children to do work around the house, it was to help them learn about the world of money. Be careful if you do choose to link the two. You may end up withholding their allowance so often they don't get much of a chance to explore. In that case, the odd time they do get it, there's a good chance they'll be so annoyed about the chores that they spend their money in reaction to *that* feeling, specifically purchasing things they know you won't like, looking to annoy you in return—there's no real learning about money in that situation. What they're learning in that power struggle is something else entirely.

That doesn't mean you can't offer to pay them to do some tasks around the house that need doing, say, those you don't have the time to do at the moment so you're happy to pay someone to do them, from a cleaning service to a handyman to an eager child. Just don't hold the money hostage: make the offer, and if they choose to do the job, pay them. A simple transaction. "Thanks!" It's a great way for them to earn extra money, especially if they're saving for something in particular, and for you to get some additional stuff done around the house.

So, I wanted my children to have a basic amount of money to play with. Remember, the best learning feels like play. What next? Interestingly, having their own money helps remove you from the equation when they want to purchase something. That means they aren't always asking you if they can have something—casting you in the role of judge, pronouncing verdicts of "yes" or "no". They have the control and the choice—they do the real thinking. And the real learning.

If you're going to the grocery store or the mall or the bookstore, remind them to bring their money (or their debit card). If they find something they'd like, help them figure out if they have enough money to pay for it. If they don't, chat about the options. Help them figure out how long it would take to save up for it. If they're close, you can talk about lending them the money now to cover the rest of the cost and then taking that amount out of their next allowance. If you have some leeway in your general budget, you could choose to say that and offer to pay the rest. There aren't hard and fast rules—it's about exploring money and possibilities together. You're trying to *help* them reach their goals.

Sometimes parents have a hard time with their children making what they deem to be frivolous purchases. But what a great way for the kids to be able to play with the concept of cost versus satisfaction versus quality—before the cost of "toys" gets significantly higher! And when they choose to make impulse buys they are also getting the chance to see how they play out. Do they play with the toy when they get home? Are they still playing with it a couple days later? A couple weeks later? How does it feel when they spend money on one thing today, only to discover they don't have enough left for something they find the next day? Is there a relationship between cost and quality? Which kinds of toys often break soon after they get home?

There are a wide range of stores to explore too, from commercial malls, to chain stores, to locally-owned stores, to dollar stores, to thrift stores; online stores and eBay and Craigslist. There are so many opportunities for learning when they have the time and some money to make choices. The overall amount doesn't matter much either—that's dependent on family circumstances. What does matter is the freedom to explore. That's where the learning is.

Money topics weave through our lives just like food and sleep do—they are an integral part of living. When topics come up, unschooling children are poised and ready to learn—just be careful not to *avoid* conversations. Fears about money can lead us to give vague answers and quickly change the topic. If you're uncomfortable, examine that. If you don't know the answer, learn alongside them! That's the beauty of unschooling. Be open and share and explore and learn.

How Does Your Child Like to Learn?

Conventionally, there is a separation between academic skills, taught by schools, and life skills, taught by parents. Yet more and more parents are feeling a time crunch and are encouraging schools to take responsibility for teaching their children life skills beyond academics, like health, character, and sex education.

As unschooling parents, we choose to retain the responsibility for all our children's learning, academic *and* life skills. Unschooling encompasses the whole range of learning that goes into being a person, a human being.

Being (noun): existence, journey, living, life, presence, vitality, essence, self, soul, spirit, substance.

How does unschooling support all that? If fitting into the school system isn't your child's "job," if living is the focus, what does the business of being human look like day-to-day?

Certainly being human looks different for everyone because each of us is a unique combination of cells—we have our own personalities, our own emotional landscape, our own physiology, our own ways of learning. And then there's how we relate to our environment: our community, our family. We each have our own ways of connecting and interacting. The beauty of unschooling is that we recognize that uniqueness, we celebrate it. We support our children as they explore their personal makeup and how they fit into the world, learning all the while.

That's another idea fundamental to unschooling: humans are born to learn. We *want* to make sense of the world around us.

Instead of seeing childhood for learning and adulthood for living, unschoolers see learning as an integral part of living regardless of your age. Unschoolers go about their day open to the world around them. They are curious. They notice things. They seek things out. They actively gather information about the world around them. That is the mindset that unschooling parents cultivate. When we open up the idea of learning beyond the teacher-student/classroom paradigm, we discover many different ways that our children go about learning.

Conventionally, these varying ways are grouped into three basic learning styles: visual; auditory; kinesthetic. Schools try to accommodate them, though the classroom environment definitely favours auditory learners. Unschooling has the freedom to genuinely support any and all ways of learning. As an unschooling parent you don't need to be an expert in the current academic model being used to describe learning theory. Instead, you have your children in front of you. Watch *them*.

That's the key. How do *they* like to learn? When you're new to unschooling, this is a great thing to focus on. Think of this deschooling time as a season of Saturdays and, as you're spending time with your children, notice how they gather information from the world around them. Challenge yourself to be open to whatever you see. Don't try to filter your observations through learning style labels: drop any preconceived notions of what learning "should" look like, and discover what it *does* look like, for *your* children.

For example, we probably know how we like to learn, but there's a good chance our children have a different style. The first part of the learning process is gathering information. Maybe we love to read about our interests, and they love to be hands-on, playing around. Or to listen to others as they talk about a topic or idea.

Think about a story and the ways it can be conveyed to an audience: through a book, words on a page to be read; through a storyteller, to be listened to, maybe with eyes closed; or through a play or movie, acted out physically. All are wonderful ways to connect an audience with a story. If we personally favour one way over another, that's cool! But that doesn't mean the other styles of storytelling aren't just as valuable to others. If we look at our children's lives through the filter of what learning looks like for us, we can easily miss seeing the learning our children are doing in their own ways. And if we don't recognize our children's day-to-day learning, it can be hard to build trust in unschooling.

Yet once we discover the ways *they* like to gather information, we are much more able to connect them to the world as they prefer to experience it. Whether it's books and websites, museums and hands-on workshops, movies and plays, podcasts and audiobooks, they are all wonderful ways to explore the world, none better than any other, except to an individual. Each of your children will have their preferences, those experiences they get the most out of; i.e., the ones they more strongly connect with and hence learn from the most. *That* is their style.

There's also a good chance you'll discover that your children's learning styles aren't as cut and dried as the labels imply. Human beings are more complex than that. In fact, it's likely that your child will enjoy more than one way of gathering information and experiencing the world. And you may see their preferred style change over time. It's the *individual* that matters, not fitting into a label.

By bringing information about the world to your children through various mediums you are helping them explore and discover which ways of gathering information work better for them. You're helping them learn how *they* like to learn. Not as a student or child, but as a person. Priceless.

Think, Think, Think ...

Learning is at the heart of unschooling—learning and living are beautifully intertwined. As human beings we *want* to make sense of our world; it's uncomfortable when we don't understand what's happening around us. So once our children have gathered information, the next step is to process it, to connect it with what they already know to build that bigger picture.

Let's look at a more detailed breakdown of conventional learning styles: visual-spatial; auditory; kinesthetic; verbal / linguistic; logical / mathematical; social / interpersonal; solitary / intrapersonal. In my mind, the first three focus on the first step of the learning process, gathering information. The additional four focus on the second step, processing information.

Processing information—thinking—is all about taking information that we've gathered and integrating it into our existing understanding of the world, building that bigger picture. And just as there are many ways to gather information, there are also many ways we might choose to process that information.

I personally favour internal, or intrapersonal (within one's self) processing. I take in information and typically prefer to think it through on my own, having conclusions close at hand before I choose talk with others about the topic. My husband, on the other hand, is more of a verbal or external processor. He starts talking about a topic from the get-go, often sharing thoughts as they occur to him.

It can be challenging when your styles differ. It took me some time to realize that in our conversations my husband was not sharing considered conclusions but rather his interim thoughts and what ifs as he processed out loud. It can be hard for internal ponderers to give external speculators the space to process their thoughts out loud without feeling like they are being provoked into an argument. But it is so helpful to understand what's going on, to shift to being a sounding board, letting the conversations unfold without trying to direct the other person's thoughts. That's important because real understanding, and learning, happens when *they* make the connections, not when they're being told what the answer is. And vice versa: if you're a verbal processor it can be challenging to be patient through the quiet times as the other person ponders, not really knowing what they're thinking until they are ready to share.

As unschooling parents it's important that we understand and support both styles and the range in between. For example, one of my children shows a preference for verbal processing, so when they express a wish for something I often help them dig into it, asking questions, helping them explore their motivation and nail down what they're looking for. More learning.

Another of my children is a strong internal processor, so when they express a wish for something, my response is more often "Sure!" I know they've already done a lot of thinking before sharing this choice so let's get going and see how it plays out. More learning.

Another thinks best when moving. Long walks in the forest, or tracing a room-to-room track in the house, the repetitive motion helps to organize their thoughts and sink deeply into reflection: to think.

Just remember, our styles aren't carved in stone. Maybe after a short conversation you realize your typically verbal/social processing child is already quite certain about the path forward they'd like to take—join them and move forward, or your continued questions may begin to feel like an interrogation. Or maybe as you quickly start down the path your typically internal/solitary processing child suggested, they start to question it—step back and join them in conversation if they're interested, or give them more time to reconsider. Either way they are learning more about themselves.

It's fun to notice how these dynamics play out in groups where people are learning, online or in person. You probably won't even notice the internal processors at first, until they're feeling ready to speak up, while the external processors are busily asking question after question, gathering and processing information in plain sight. Again, no one method is better than another, except to an individual.

Another interesting observation I've made over the years about the learning process is that unschooling children seem to find that learning sweet spot of being "in the flow" more often than their conventionally schooled counterparts. You know that feeling, yes? When you're so into the task at hand that time seems to stand still? Where you don't second guess yourself; in fact, you don't analyze yourself at all—you just *do.* Unschooling children are free to follow their curiosity, to immerse themselves in their interests, so it's understandable that they are more often engaged in these beautiful moments of flow. There is *so* much learning found there, both about the world and about themselves.

By giving your children the space to play with how they process the information they gather, by being a responsive partner in the dance of questions and conversations and silences as they piece together their unique picture of the world and how it works, you are helping them explore and discover how *they* like to learn. And with that deep understanding of themselves, they will be better able to choose and create environments for living and learning and working that are a good fit for them, throughout their lifetime.

Supporting Our Unschooling Children

Reader Question:

I would love to hear your take on unschooling in a co-operative circumstance. How much "getting out of the way" and how much instigating would you encourage? I know all kids and families are different, but isn't it just as much our responsibility to teach kids how to work together, respect each other and learn through organized activities?

There are so many facets to this lovely question. To organize my answer a bit, I pulled out four ideas that it touches on and discussed them from an unschooling perspective.

How Much "Getting out of the Way"

versus "Instigating"

First, let's look at the question of "how much." That little phrase is so interesting! And it's so understandable to want to have some guidelines when we are first getting our feet wet with something as unconventional as unschooling. We love to measure things and see how well we're doing. Yet unschooling really isn't about external measures, like the number of occasions you steered clear of or instigated activities—it's about *your children's* needs. If you find yourself tempted to look to the clock to measure you involvement with your children by time, or to count questions answered or activities attended outside the home each week, catch yourself, breathe, and look to your children. Are *they* curious and engaged with life? In good spirits? That's your measure.

As for the question of "getting out of the way" or "instigating," your children will let you know how much they would like you to be involved. If they are immersed in an activity, not asking you questions or wanting your help, that's probably a stay-out-of-the-way kind of moment. Yet "getting out of the way" doesn't mean being uninvolved. When those moments happened, I did my own thing but I stayed nearby, careful to respond to questions or requests quickly so as to help them stay in the flow of their activity. I'd unobtrusively bring drinks or food when I thought they might be needed. I would support their intense engagement and learning by not interfering with it.

And then there were other times, moments when they seemed to be between activities, or looking for something new. In those moments I'd mention some things I'd come across recently that I thought they might enjoy until one caught their attention, or inspired another idea of their own. "I found this board game at the yard sale down the street. It looks like fun! Wanna play?" Or "The other day a friend linked to this new website with games I think you'd like. Here, I'll show you." Or "Shall we go to the library and look for pirate books?"

If after a few ideas nothing seemed to catch their attention, that was a clue that maybe they were looking for some down time to hang out and *be* for a while—they don't always have to be doing. Maybe we'd watch a favourite movie, or do some baking together, or take a walk. I'd look for slower pace activities we could do together that would allow for conversations to blossom, or give them the space for internal processing to happen, whether or not they wanted to actually talk about it. Again, it's about following their clues.

Looking at the Concept of "Instigating"

To me, those were (and are) instigating moments—opportunities for me to bring new things into their lives, or to create a comfortable and inviting space to slow down in a world that prizes busyness. I have the feeling though, that most people have a stronger characterization of "instigating," so let's dig in a bit deeper.

When it comes to instigating, I think it's all about your motivation. My handy online thesaurus helps me make this point: the words encouraging and persuading are both synonyms for instigating. Yet the motivations behind encouragement and persuasion can be very different—it's a subtle, but important, distinction. Important because our motivation influences our actions.

With unschooling in mind, I think of instigating or encouraging as bringing interesting things to their attention: "Cassy, there's an exhibit of landscape paintings by local artists this month. I know how much you love painting trees—do you want to go on Thursday?" It's about bringing something to their attention that you sincerely think they might enjoy. That's an example of the influence you can have in the relationship once you've developed yourself as a trustworthy source of information. And in the realm of encouragement and influence, "no, thanks" is always a fine answer. The motivation here is to support *Cassy's interest in painting.*

Persuasion isn't quite so amenable to a connected relationship: "Cassy, there's an exhibit of landscape paintings by local artists this month. You'll learn how to paint trees better—you want to improve your painting, right? We're free Thursday, we'll go then." Here there is definitely pressure on Cassy to go. In fact, there's really no opening to say "no, thanks" without belittling her own interest in painting. The motivation here is to support the *parent's interest in teaching Cassy* to paint trees. And further, if Cassy isn't interested, when they do go, she's not likely going to learn much. It's more likely she'll be complaining and/or watching the clock to see when she can leave.

Which way better supports Cassy's real learning? And their relationship?

With unschooling, instigating isn't about pressuring or coercing your children to do something with an end goal of your own in mind. It's about bringing something to their attention that you think they might enjoy—*their enjoyment* is the goal. That's because we know their learning is rampant when they're having fun.

Once you are adept at reading your children and understanding what they're up to in the moment, they will give you pretty clear clues as to how involved they'd like you to be throughout the day. Just remember, with unschooling, "instigating" shouldn't be veiled attempts at "teaching." Which leads us nicely to the next idea.

What Is Meant by "Our Responsibility to Teach Kids"

Going back to the idea that the words we use (even in our heads) are important because our thoughts influence our perspective and actions, pay special attention when using the word "teach." When you catch it in your internal dialogue, that's a clue to dig deeper into those thoughts. To understand unschooling more deeply, it's important to make the distinction between teaching and learning—they are two completely different acts. We're interested in our children's *learning.*

When we look for our children's learning in their everyday activities, we begin to see all the learning that happens as they go about their day, without *any* teaching. And it's real learning, learning that makes sense and is re-membered, precisely because it came up naturally. It was part of the puzzle of the moment as they strode toward their goal—whether that was building a block tower, play-ing a board game, reading a video game guide, or reorgan-izing their bedroom.

The other interesting phrase is "our responsibility." It's worth taking some time to think about that idea too. Our responsibility to whom? To society? I remember these conversations with myself as I was learning about un-schooling! Certainly most parents who choose this lifestyle for their family aren't approaching it as an excuse to shirk "our responsibility to raise decent human beings," though when people first learn about the kinds of things unschoolers do (or don't do) sometimes it can appear that way—until they understand the principles behind it. As I thought more about this, I realized that I had even higher goals for my parenting than society in general did, which led to the realization that if I focused on the responsibility I felt *to my children*, in the end I'd more than meet any responsibility I felt to society, and that phrase soon withered out of my vocabulary.

"Work Together, Respect Each Other, and Learn through Organized Activities"

And finally, let's take a moment to look at these goals. They sound pretty reasonable, don't they? Things that many adults do? Yet is teaching really the way to go? Following the last section, let's look at these from the perspective of learning.

How might our children learn these kinds of skills? Through experience. And that's real learning, learning that makes sense to them because it's playing out right in front of them, *not* them being told how to behave beforehand and then trying to remember that in the moment.

Using the "how to work together" example, they'll be noticing the other kids' goals and behaviours, their own feelings surrounding the situation, what their goals are and how they'd like to see things move forward. It's at *that* time that information we share about ways to analyze and work through the situation will make sense and be helpful.

It's a dance that you and your children will get better at as you get to know each other more deeply—they will be open to chat about the situation, to think about how their goals differ and how they are similar, to imagine ways they might all be met, to evaluate how important things are to them, and to think about ways they might choose to compromise. And then there's the whole negotiating piece, working with the others involved to come up with a plan they are all willing to follow to accomplish the work together. They are gaining experience with skills that will be useful over their lifetime.

The next example given was about teaching kids respect for each other. Think of the people you respect. I suspect that respect was *not* taught—it was *earned* through behaviour and actions over time. Is respect really something you can teach or demand? You can certainly work towards being civil to one another (if that's an issue), but that's different than respect.

The last example was about teaching kids to learn through organized activities. Again, that's a reasonable question for people newer to unschooling! The conventional idea of learning through organized (meaning adult-run) activities is so ingrained in our society that it's valued above so many other ways of learning. And sure, some kids will enjoy that format—*if* they are interested in the activity. My kids have certainly enjoyed some organized activities over the years, but it's not the only way to learn.

And it's not a more important way over any other way. It's dependent on the child. Again, look to your children.

The first thing to ask yourself is whether it's an activity they are interested in. Sure, you might encourage your child to try something out because you're pretty sure they will enjoy it once they go even though right now they are hesitant. But a well-connected relationship allows that to happen without the child feeling undue pressure and it takes time to get there. Watch your child.

Once their interest is established, then it's a question of whether it's an environment they enjoy. When we first checked out Michael's dojo years ago, I mentioned there were other dojos around and if he didn't enjoy the class, we could try others. Find the environment that works for your child, don't try to mould your child to fit the environment.

It always comes back to watching and supporting the child, doesn't it?

Yes.

This determined support for your children as they explore the world and how they tick blossoms into a strong and well-connected relationship, a deep level of mutual trust and respect, and an incredible amount of learning that no generalized curriculum could envision.

It is the heart of unschooling.

Learning Is Learning No Matter Your Age

... Or helping the reluctant spouse/partner/other significant adult in your child's life learn about unschooling.

It's pretty typical that one parent takes on the bulk of responsibility for the minutiae of day-to-day parenting. Maybe one parent is working out of the home and one parent is unschooling with the children, though there are lots of different takes on that theme: maybe both are working outside the home and they alternate their hours; maybe the parent earning the bulk of the income works from home; maybe it's a single parent working from home or using some child care, but with an ex in the mix.

Regardless of the circumstances, it's understandable that it's the parent who dives in and learns about homeschooling and unschooling who becomes more and more interested in moving the family in that direction. Often the spouse/partner agrees to try it out for a while, not understanding it very deeply, but trusting the more informed parent. Yet if one parent has taken the bulk of responsibility for learning about and implementing unschooling in the family, chances are the other parent will eventually start to wonder what's going on. Maybe parenting philosophies seem to be changing and they puzzle over how they fit in. Maybe they start to worry about their children's learning—that's not surprising, they can't find the school-type learning they are likely looking for anywhere!

On the other hand, it's probably an exciting time for the unschooling-focused parent. You're understanding unschooling more and more deeply and you can see the positive effects this lifestyle is having on you and your children. Maybe you're also feeling a bit frustrated that your spouse/partner isn't seeing it too—you want them to learn quickly and join you in your growing excitement. Try to breathe through and release that. Be mindful not to fall into the role of teacher, doling out a reading list to be completed, the test being life under your watchful eyes. It won't help your spouse learn any faster and will probably cause lots of frustration in the relationship.

Keep putting yourself back in the mindset that you're not trying to convince them, to teach them. You're trying to help them learn. Sound familiar? With unschooling, when we look at learning the focus is on the learner, not on the teacher. It's not about you, it's about them. Look at things through *their* eyes; understand where they're coming from. They care about their children. They want what's best for them. Meet them where they are. What are they curious about right now? How can you support their learning about unschooling?

Well, how do they learn best? Unschooling is based on universal and lifelong learning principles, meaning there aren't separate ways for children and adults to learn. You've discovered your kids have their preferred ways of learning things—adults do too. So don't be tempted to overwhelm your spouse/partner with information in the way *you* like to learn. Share the information you think they would find helpful, in the format and amount that best supports *their* learning style.

If they are keen readers and want to dive into the details, feel free to share the websites and forums and email lists and books you've likely been devouring for months. Maybe they'll read, ask questions, and great conversations will ensue. But if they aren't interested in learning that way, remember that's not a slight against you, any more than it is when your kids don't take you up on an offer. You're learning more about how your spouse likes to learn. And it's to your advantage as the primary unschooling parent to help your spouse/partner understand what you're up to, so devote some of your time and energy to making that learning as easy as possible for them.

As you know, there are lots of ways to learn things! And when does learning typically best happen? When it makes a connection with some knowledge or question they already have or when they're particularly curious about something. So notice when a piece of information about unschooling might make a connection for them.

Is there a particular issue or question your spouse/partner has right now? Let's pick a topic, say video games, and brainstorm some ways you can share information over the next while to help them discover all the learning that your child's doing while playing:

- Share information that directly connects to the question: sometimes sharing information online— by email, message, etc.—is less emotionally charged than face-to-face discussions. You could forward a related unschooling discussion email, a forum post, or a link to a web page, maybe with a short preface from you about how it relates to your current discussions: "We were chatting about video games and learning the other night and I came across this information you might find interesting." Not a long and drawn-out treatise citing a dozen sources—you're not trying to overwhelm them, you're trying to help them learn. Share in digestible bites.

- Point out related moments in your lives as they happen: "Hey look, Todd is reading through his game guide, figuring out how to beat the boss he's stuck on." Maybe they don't notice those moments on their own, caught up in their own things.

- Invite your spouse/partner to get directly involved: "Todd and I are trying to figure out this puzzle he's stuck on, can you help us?" Hands on observations can be really helpful in seeing the learning that is happening. Even better, ask him to play! Often parents don't realize how much quick thinking and analysis is going on during game play until they try it themselves and all of sudden have to manage their health level, their map location, and their weapons, all the while trying to quickly determine the most effective moves to make.

- Is there a book on the topic you think they'd find particularly helpful? If they don't like to read, what about an audiobook? More and more books have audio editions and they might be a great fit with driving to work or while doing work around the house.

If there's not a particular issue, you might want to generally help them feel involved and engaged in everyone's day-to-day lives. You could snap and send a few pictures during the day, letting them see what you're up to and including a brief description. Or you could put that information on a blog, even making it invite only so you share what the kids are up to only with close family. If you think they'd benefit from seeing other unschooling families in action, maybe find an unschooling gathering or conference through an online group with whom you feel a connection. If you have a local group, maybe set up a weekend park day so that more spouses/partners are able to attend.

The key is to share your lives with them so they feel connected, so they can see firsthand that their children aren't being neglected but are living and learning and growing and thriving. Don't expect it to happen overnight. Remember, they are likely to have less time each day to devote to learning about unschooling—but they are still fully devoted to being a parent.

And remember to support *all* their learning. Certainly about unschooling, but also about anything else they're interested in. If they have a hobby, happily support that, just as you would your children's interests. Listen to them share their joy. Share with them related things you think they might find interesting: an article online, a magazine you found at the store, a documentary you found on Netflix. Not only are those are nice and loving things to do, they are also real examples of unschooling in action.

Show them how unschooling works, don't just tell them. Because learning is learning no matter your age.

CHAPTER EIGHT

:: unconventional ::

Unschooling is decidedly unconventional.

"Learn to Say No or You'll Spoil Your Child"

"to impair, damage, or harm the character or nature of (someone) by unwise treatment, excessive indulgence, etc.: *to spoil a child by pampering him.*" ~ dictionary.com

A "spoiled" child is one that exhibits behaviour problems as a result of overindulgence by his or her parents. And in the mainstream world of parenting, it's a strong condemnation. The challenge for unschooling parents is that when people first hear about the kind of parenting that goes hand in hand with unschooling—responding quickly to their children's needs, paying attention to them, conversing *with* them, saying yes more often and so on—their first thought is often "but that kind of parenting will spoil a child."

Is that true? Will unschooling spoil a child?

What Does a "Spoiled" Child Look Like?

Being "spoiled" is a derogatory label that describes a generalized judgment. Typical descriptions of the constellation of behaviours that lead people to label a child "spoiled" include: is rude, throws tantrums when they don't get their way, refuses to share, acts bossy, ignores parents/adults questions and instructions, refuses to go to bed.

Basically, these children have come to expect to get their way most, if not all, of the time. They feel *entitled* to get their way. And to ensure they get their way, they have learned how to manipulate others through these kinds of negative behaviours.

Why Doesn't an Unschooling Child "Spoil"?

Sometimes the actions of unschooling parents may *appear* to be very similar to the conventional dynamic of children being "spoiled" by their parents, but the motivations behind them are different. These negative behaviours develop when parents do so much for their children, so often, that the children learn to expect these things to be done *for them.* Unschooling parents do a lot to support their children, but do so with an eye to helping their children do things *for themselves.*

This changes the perspective of *all* the conversations unschooling parents have with their children and creates a completely different parent-child relationship. Unschooling children are learning very different things from their parents' actions.

Let's look at some examples of parenting actions, the conventional and unschooling motivations behind those actions, and what the children likely learn as a result.

Give their children material things.
- conventional motivation: to motivate/control their children's behaviour with rewards (children learn to expect to receive things regularly)
- unschooling motivation: to help their children get the things they are interested in (children learn their interests are valued)

Do things their children want.
- conventional motivation: to avoid confrontation—want their children to like them (children learn to expect to get their way)
- unschooling motivation: to listen to their children's input—open to changing their minds (children learn their thoughts and feelings are valued)

Don't punish negative behaviour.
- conventional motivation: to avoid confrontation—want their children to like them (children learn to expect to get their way)
- unschooling motivation: to talk with their children to understand the reasons behind the behaviours (children learn to understand themselves and explore other ways to meet their needs)

Respond to their children's distress.
- conventional motivation: to get them to be quiet and move on (children learn yelling/crying is a good tool to quickly get what they want)
- unschooling motivation: to help their children move through the distressing situation (children learn they have their parents' support and help)

Because the parent's motivations behind these actions are so different the conversations that ensue between the parent and child are also very different, and hence what the child learns from the experience is very different.

A Different Approach to Developing Responsibility

Unschooling parents also dedicate their time to helping their children take as much responsibility as they want.

What does that look like in real life? Let's imagine a five-year-old who wants to make cookies.

In an unschooling home, chances are the parent will act in support of their child: they'll read through the recipe with them; they'll pay attention to whether the child is interested in gathering all the tools and ingredients, patiently pointing out where all the stuff is located if that's the case, and if not, quickly gathering the supplies on the counter; they'll show the child which buttons to press or dials to turn on the stove to set the temperature and turn it on; they'll sit back as the child measures out ingredients—answering questions, maybe chatting about what the different ingredients do; they'll watch, again patiently, as the child stirs the ingredients together, giggling with them as the loose flour makes a cloud, and taking over the mixing for a bit if the child gets tired and wants some help; when putting the dough on the cookie sheets, if their child wants to try making a really big cookie alongside the more regular-sized ones, they'll might say "what a fun idea!" and help them figure out the best way to bake it; and as the cookies bake, parent and child may have fun playing with bubbles in the sink as they wash the dishes used. In other words, the unschooling parent follows their child's lead throughout the process to see how much or how little they'd like their parent to be hands-on in the process. The goal isn't the cookies—it's the child's exploration and learning. Not only of the task at hand, but of thinking things through in general, of actions and outcomes.

In a conventional home, chances are things will go quite differently. The parent will probably direct the child's actions more, with the goal being to teach the child how to properly make cookies. There's a recipe to follow so there's no room for exploration—getting it right is the key goal. The parent will probably turn on the oven, "you're too young to touch the stove." They may also gather all the supplies and ingredients, "we don't have all day." And they'll be constantly and closely monitoring the process, judging it, directing it, even taking over at times: "here's how you make sure the measuring spoon is full"; "don't stir too fast, you'll make a mess"; "make sure the cookies are all the same size."

In both families, those dynamics play out over the years in many diverse situations, with unschooling parents focused on helping their child learn how to evaluate situations and make choices and take as much responsibility as they are interested in, and with conventional parents more focused on doing things quickly and "right" and getting their children to do what they're told in pursuit of those goals. But by constantly doing things for their children, over their children's wishes, their children come to believe that they *aren't* capable, that others *should* be doing things for them. That they are *entitled* to have things done for them. Not to mention, how many people would choose to step up and do things knowing their performance will be judged critically?

What to Do?

When we place adult-sized expectations (of both speed and skill) on our children's actions, we miss discovering how much children really *want* to participate in life, to do things they see the adults around them doing, to the very best of their ability.

Given a family environment where parents consistently step in and do things because they can do them faster (they have busy lives) and/or "better" (meaning to their own adult standards), where parents use material objects as rewards (and take them away as punishment) to try to control their children's behaviour, and do whatever they can to avoid confrontation and distress, it's unsurprising that the children's wish to actively participate in life is extinguished and these kinds of "spoiled" negative behaviours develop.

The conventional answer to this issue is to counsel parents to stand their ground—to not allow themselves to be manipulated by their children. And the power struggles go round and round.

But if that's not the relationship you want to develop with your children, instead of putting up a wall of defense against their pleas, spend even *more* time with them. Get to know them better, to understand them better. As you unwrap the mystery of each of your children, their challenging behaviour in various situations will no longer seem inexplicable or manipulative—it will begin to make sense and you'll be able to help them explore other ways to move through those situations.

Instead of closing down and throwing demands and expectations *at* their children, unschooling parents choose to open up and have conversations *with* their children.

Unschooling will *not* spoil a child.

"If You're Bored, I'll Give You Something to Do"

I imagine most of us heard some version of this growing up. It was a kind of threat—that "something to do" was something your parent was sure you wouldn't want to do, a household chore like tidying up your room or cleaning the bathroom or taking out the garbage. The underlying message was received loud and clear: keep yourself busy.

And it goes beyond expressing boredom. When a parent sees a child "just" sitting around on the couch they'll often comment, "Nothing to do? I can find you something to do." Their train of thought broken, the child likely replies, "No, I'm busy," and goes to their room to find something to do, or to at least appear to be busy.

Why Is Busyness Prized?

Being busy is a badge of honour in our society: if you're not busy, you're lazy. Parents share their schedules, trying to one-up each other: "Between hockey practice and games for Bill, and dance classes and girl guides for Robin, the only night we're home is Sunday. Which we spend helping them with their homework and getting organized for the next week." To which the reply may well be, "Nice! I *wish* we had Sunday off!"

It probably shouldn't have been so surprising to me then that, as a young teen, the typical response my daughter received when acquaintances found out she didn't go to school was, "You don't go to school? What do you do all day? Aren't you bored?" They were so used to being told what to do they had a hard time imagining anything else.

Have an Interest? Take lessons!

Another contributor to the world of busyness is that so many parents see organized lessons as the only way to pursue an interest. Their child loves video games? Programming camp! Dances around the house? Ballet lessons. Loves to sing along with the radio? Singing lessons. Enjoys kicking the ball around? Soccer league. And so it goes. If a child expresses any interest in something, parents immediately jump to lessons.

Dancing around the house and singing to the radio don't *count*. There's no teacher around, so what could they be learning? Yet unschooling parents understand that their children are learning a *lot* through their own exploration. In fact, the learning found by following their own unique path of connections through a topic is often stronger than the learning found by following a generic curriculum path.

So though organized lessons and sports leagues give parents "proof" that their children are learning and busy, they also have a couple of downsides. When a child's keen interest in something is turned over to formal lessons or a league, the child loses control. Their excitement may quickly fade as their interest is co-opted by the mundane routine of organization—practices on Wednesday and games on Saturday; work on this piece of music this week. The joy of play is replaced by resistance to practice.

Another downside is that all these organized extra-curricular activities have left children little time for free play. Okay, a lot of parents might call that an upside: "they are safe, being watched over by an adult"; "it keeps them out of trouble." But there is an incredible amount of learning to be found in free play that many children are missing out on. Peter Gray is a strong advocate of play. In his book *Free to Learn: Why Unleashing the Instinct to Play Will Make Our Children Happier, More Self-Reliant, and Better Students for Life*, he defines play as "nature's way of teaching children how to solve their own problems, control their impulses, modulate their emotions, see from others' perspectives, negotiate differences, and get along with others as equals." Unschoolers see that definition in action every day.

That's not to say organized activities are "bad." I don't think they're very helpful when the goal is to be busy, but they can be a wonderful experience when the activity is the child's *choice.* Choice is key. If they want to participate, if they are enjoying themselves, that's great! Talk with them. Help them explore not only their interests, but also how those interests fit into their lives. Happily, unschooling families don't have the time commitments of a school schedule, so they have a lot more time to play around with.

Time to Think

So if the goal is busy, then "not busy" is the adversary. Yet "not busy" is really the only time we get to think, to process, to contemplate. The challenge is that we have nothing to show others for the time investment, no proof of accomplishment. And besides, society imagines, what does a child really have to think about?

A lot.

Unschooling parents have a lot of respect for the process of thinking, for the time that takes and the space that it needs. Contemplation and introspection are an integral part of the learning process, even though they can't be measured or tested. It's how the bigger picture of life comes together. It's in those times that connections are found between seemingly disparate bits of life, illuminating them both a bit more. It's how people, children and adults alike, figure out who they are, and who they want to be.

Time to think doesn't necessarily mean sitting still in silence. In my family it's looked like many afternoons spent on the swing in our yard, or wandering through the forest. It's looked like the soothing and repetitive nature of a video game, building experience encounter by encounter, or a marathon of episodes of a well-loved TV show. Sometimes it's hours spent in their rooms, reading or napping or re-organizing.

It needn't always be about the doing.

The time to think and wonder and *be* is so important.

"You Have to Limit Screen Time"

Before we dive in, let's take a moment to look at the phrase "screen time." It lumps together devices that involve a visual interface: TVs, video games, computers, cell phones, e-readers, tablets, etc. Yet we use them to do so many diverse things, from entertainment to communication to learning, that to lump them altogether as "screens" seems thoughtless and demeaning.

If we want to categorize them, I think "technology" would work better. Technology is fast becoming ubiquitous in our lives, yet it's still all so new. I've seen the advent of all these personal devices in my lifetime (okay, not black and white TV, that was a bit before my time, but I remember our first colour television set). That's a *lot* of change in a handful decades.

"Zoning Out"

Let's talk about TV as it is the longest lived in the group.. You've probably heard parents worriedly discuss how their children "zone out" when they watch TV. And they aren't wrong—that's probably what they see happening in front of them. Yet, that behaviour is not what I, nor other unschoolers, typically see when our children watch TV. Why the discrepancy? I imagine that it's because this "zoning out" behaviour isn't caused by watching TV, but is the result of other things in their lives that lead them to use TV as a tool to de-stress.

It's hard for conventional parents to imagine that the TV experience might be significantly different for unschooling families just because our lifestyles are different. Yet unschooling parents are explicitly working to set up a home and learning environment with minimal stress. As a result, unschooling children aren't usually watching TV to escape or relax, they are most often watching with *purpose*. They are actively *engaged*—they don't look like "zombies."

One of the reasons for that is that unschooling children choose when and what they watch. They aren't watching because they're allowed an hour between five and six p.m. so by golly they'll use that hour to watch whatever they can find. They are watching because there is something they *want* to watch. Maybe they're paying rapt attention. Maybe they are asking questions. Maybe they are pausing and looking things up. Their parents are often *with* them—answering questions, laughing at the jokes, sharing observations, and looking things up themselves. That doesn't mean unschooling children never watch TV to unwind, to process experiences in a comforting environment—that's wonderfully okay. But those experiences are transitory, not the norm.

Learning about Themselves

I think what this notion of limiting screen time really boils down to is parents wanting to help their children figure out how to weave into their lives the multitude of choices we have available today.

And that's a wonderful idea—understanding our-selves and our activity choices is a key piece of life's puzzle. But to try to accomplish that through rules and limits isn't really about helping them learn about *themselves*; that's more about expecting them to adhere to someone else's ideal of who they *should* be.

Unschooling parents are choosing to support their children as they learn about themselves. And as part of that, unschooling parents realize that the frequency, dura-tion, and variety of activities that feels good for each of us, is unique to each of us. So without rules to fall back on, how do unschooling parents help their children discover what that might look like for them? By supporting their exploration.

Those experiences will include lots of times when their children choose and enjoy activities, and then move on. There will also be times when their children will begin to feel frustrated. The kids may choose to stop the activity, and other times they may want to push through the frus-tration to accomplish their goal.

Unschooling parents notice these moments and help their children process and learn from those experiences—we don't leave them to figure it all out on their own. How did it feel? What was the goal? What was the cost? When did you notice things were getting out-of-sorts?

Balance as Steadiness

I don't really like to call this process finding *balance* because most people tend to focus on the definition of "equal distribution; state of equilibrium," rather than the one of "mental steadiness or emotional stability." It's that focus on the equal distribution of activities that leads to timing things and creating limits: "You've watched TV for an hour, now go outside and play." Balance isn't necessarily about equality.

I think it's more useful to focus on the idea of steadiness and stability—the activities themselves don't matter much, it's their impact on the person doing them. This perspective helps us focus on our children's understanding of themselves, on their exploration of the kinds of activities and how much of them they enjoy and that contribute to their feeling steady and whole and comfortable.

Through experience, they learn how their activity choices depend on both the situation at hand and how they're feeling in the moment. They discover the clues their body and mind are giving them that signal that a change of activity would be welcome. When we limit things for others, they get little opportunity to hear those signals.

How We Can Help

The really interesting thing is that parents are also figuring out how to weave technology into *their* lives alongside their children—it's new to us too! Here's a tip: don't berate yourself if, in hindsight, you wish you had made a different choice—shame and guilt aren't great motivators for anyone, so they don't make great examples for your children.

Instead, share observations: "Wow, I just noticed the time; I ended up on the computer longer than I planned." Share what you observe in yourself. How that might differ from your goals. The ways you try to bring your goals and your activities into alignment. How your goals may shift as you gain experience.

None of this sharing needs to be done in long, protracted conversations, though sometimes that might happen too. Maybe they'll ask a question. Maybe they'll share an idea for you. Maybe they'll share their experiences. When they are interested, engage in discussions with them.

Another thing to consider: make other activities available and inviting. If your children are getting tired of their current activity, electronic or otherwise, but don't see other choices, they may stay where they are, getting increasingly uncomfortable, both physically and emotionally. If you notice this might be the case, again, share your observations. Short and sweet and matter-of-factly. Not judgmentally. Offer up a board game, a walk around the block, a fresh batch of playdough, a trip to the park. But don't be upset if they say "no thanks." Remember, you don't know for sure what they're thinking, what they're exploring. What you want to do is help them see the other choices available, so they remember they're making a choice.

Though it's more time consuming than setting up rules, helping our children get to know themselves to this depth is an important aspect of unschooling. Support them as they explore the ways that activities impact their physical and emotional well-being, in both positive and negative ways. Encourage them as they gain experience with making choices, discovering the clues that guide them in making choices that help them feel steady and whole and comfortable.

Unschooling is about supporting *all* the learning that goes into being human.

"Video Games Are

Making Children Violent"

The public outcry against violence in the media isn't new. It started with violence in movies and TV, and in the last twenty-odd years has grown to include video games. Yet not everyone is swayed. And in my own family's experience, and from the video game experiences I've seen shared over the last decade by countless other unschooling families, aggressive behaviour and/or acts of violence are not a foregone result of playing lots of video games.

So why the supposed correlation?

Because the majority of children play video games, so chances are an aggressive child plays them. If an issue arises with any child, it's very likely that they've played video games, so when you look at their activities you'll find them.

But let's take that a step further.

If we assume it's true that violent video game playing causes increased aggression and violence, since the majority of children are now playing violent video games, shouldn't the amount of violence committed by children be rising? That's the cause and effect relationship being put forth. But it's not.

In fact, according to the CDC, the US youth homicide rates have dropped by about 50 percent since 1994, as have youth violent crime arrests since 1995. Youth non-fatal assault injury rates have also dropped since 2001, though not as dramatically. (All these statistics are available at http://www.cdc.gov/violenceprevention/youthviolence/s tats_at-a_glance.) Any way you slice it, over the last decade or so, youth violence has dropped against a backdrop of a dramatic rise in youth playing violent video games.

Yay? Absolutely, but that's not really the point, is it?

As unschooling parents, the stats are nice to know as part of the bigger picture, but they don't define the children in front of you: *they* are what's important. However your children are choosing to spend their time, what really matters is their lives. Pay attention. What does their world look like to *them*?

When you see their activities through their eyes, you will understand why they are making the choices they do. For example, my eldest has always played a lot of video games. By spending time with him, by chatting with him often, I knew what he was getting out of the experience. And it wasn't a desensitized and violent outlook on life. For him, it was immersion in stories. What is it for your gaming child?

Not sure? Let's talk about a few ways you can support your child's interest in video games. Ways you can discover the person your child *is*, not who the statistics or society's fears say he or she will become. As in all things parenting, it's about *connecting* with your children. And staying connected.

What are some ways you can connect through video games?

Watch Them Play

This is a wonderful way to connect! What's the game about? What are they trying to do? Watch their minds in action as they solve puzzles, strategize battles, read maps, and use game currency. Cheer with them as they complete levels; commiserate with them as they try things again and again. Don't belittle the games or their efforts. Don't watch with an eye to moving them to another activity. Be there *with* them. See what they see. Revel in their joy.

Help Them

Next step—help them! Now that you have an idea of what the game is about, what are they finding challenging? Look up a guide or three online. Can't figure out how to beat that boss? Do a bit of research and share with your child strategies that other people have used. Did you see a heart piece in the corner of the screen? Point it out. Help them accomplish what they're trying to do.

Play Yourself

Now that you've seen the fun of playing and you've gotten familiar with some of the game's layout and strategies, try it! Your child will probably love helping *you* out. It's not as easy as it looks, is it? You'll probably been even more impressed with your child's skills. I know I was. Maybe you'll have found a wonderful activity to share with your children—I know quite a few unschooling parents who've thoroughly enjoyed World of Warcraft and Final Fantasy and Minecraft with their kids! Personally, my speed is more along the lines of Phoenix Wright, Animal Crossing, and Mario Party. Just this morning my eldest made a point to tell me that the newest Phoenix Wright game is out now. Care, consideration, and connection.

If you don't enjoy playing, that's okay too. You can still enjoy spending time with them, enjoy being able to understand enough to participate in conversations. You can still connect with them over video games in other ways.

Bring Interesting and Related Things to Them

So where do things stand now? Chances are, you're beginning to understand what they're talking about when they share their latest accomplishment and you can celebrate with them. You see how much they're learning as they play. And you understand *why* they enjoy playing. The shining joy in their eyes makes your eyes light up too.

I bet now you'll start to notice connections to the games they're playing as you go about your day— interesting things that you can bring to your children that they will enjoy and that will connect and expand their worlds: a Minecraft T-shirt you brought home last week and they've worn most days since; an online article detailing Animal Crossing holidays; a wiki you found about the roots of the made-up language used in their favourite game; a surprise subscription to a gaming magazine; a CD of their favourite game music; an online database of Pokémon stats; a forum you discover where they read voraciously for a while and eventually start posting.

No matter the topic—video games, TV, hockey, dinosaurs—when you build strong and connected relationships with your children, you are showing through your actions that you care about and support them. They will feel more comfortable coming to you for help when they are feeling frustrated or angry. You will notice when things get challenging, and be comfortable approaching them to share your observations, your experience, and your love and support.

I think much of society's challenges with youth behaviour stems from a deep disconnect between parents and their children. Unschooling parents are choosing to do things differently.

Chores and an Unschooling Childhood

With unschooling, we are choosing to not mould our children into our image of a perfect child, but to help them explore and learn about themselves. For that to unfold more smoothly, it helps to imagine yourself as helping them do *their* work, rather than directing it; to think of everyone as a full member of the family.

That's a good start, but I've also seen that used as a reason to insist children do chores: "You're a member of this family and this is our house, so you need to do your part to keep it up." In my experience, the big issue with this stance is that it's the parent's standard being used, not the child's, so the child is understandably resistant.

Let's dig into that a bit more. As parents, what's our goal with the whole chore thing? Maybe, getting help to meet our living standard. That seems a reasonable answer—sometimes we do need help. But probably not as often as we think. I think far more often we convince ourselves that we're asking our children to help us with the goal of *teaching them life skills*. But from what we already know about learning through unschooling, is teaching a good way to encourage *learning*?

There seemed to be a disconnect there, so I asked myself more questions. How long does it really take to learn how to clean a toilet? The real answer is, once they *want* to clean a toilet, less than five minutes. Or vacuum? Ditto. No matter how we rationalize it, chores are really about asking our children help us meet our own standard of living. Hmm ...

And then I thought some more. Would me doing the bulk of the upkeep in our home be "spoiling" them? Letting them "get away" with something? Shouldn't they be "taking responsibility" for our home? As I mulled that over, I eventually came to disagree. In fact, it dawned on me that choosing to do the work myself to meet my own standard of living *is* a good example for them of taking responsibility.

Huh? *Not* making them do chores is an example of responsibility? How? Because they know it's *my* benchmarks of cleanliness that I'm looking to meet, not theirs. (If it was theirs, *they* would be asking me to clean.) By doing the work myself I'm taking responsibility for fulfilling my own needs. But don't do it in a vacuum. Appreciate your accomplishments: "Yay! I can see the kitchen table!" Share your intentions: "This weekend I want to tidy the great room." Let them see the process in action—that's how they learn.

What this perspective also did was release any expectations I had of others. It was surprisingly freeing! And it better fit with another of my long-term goals: to support my children as they explore *their* standards and discover the environment in which *they* feel most comfortable day-to-day. Real learning about themselves that will benefit them throughout their lifetime.

And without expectations, when I do ask for their help, they can truly choose to help me. Conversely, if they feel I'm expecting their help, saying yes would also mean worrying that it could be used against them in the future ("but you vacuumed *last* week"). If that's the case, it's more likely they'll say no, even if they have the time and inclination. Without expectations, each moment is its own and everyone has a real choice.

"But the house is still messy! And I'm still frustrated!"

I'm sorry. So now let's delve into that issue—it's a *different* question.

As parents we can support our own standards in our home without imposing them on everyone else. Remember, we're looking at all the members of our family as unique individuals of differing ages. Not only will adults and children likely have different barometers for judging their environment, the adults themselves will probably have different needs too. Maybe you like it reasonably tidy, and your partner likes it completely clutter free. Or vice versa. Maybe your kids are indifferent. So if tidiness is an issue you and your partner are struggling with, first nail down exactly what's bothering each of you. That'll help you not only better explain your needs to each other, but also help you narrow in on possible solutions.

Let's say you start with the general issue, maybe something along the lines of, "I'd like to keep the house clean." From there you can ask yourself things like, is it really the whole house? Or mostly the family room where you spend most of your time? Or the kitchen? Or the bathrooms? Or the basement? Sure, it'd be nice if house elves kept them all tidy, but which room is it that actually triggers your frustration? Is it mostly the tidiness that bothers you, like clutter? Or is it cleanliness, like dirty walls or dirty dishes? Why does it bother you? Does it trigger your mom's voice in your head making you feel bad? What is actually "bad" about it? Or does the clutter make it hard for you to concentrate?

Once you've really nailed what is triggering your general "must keep the house clean" response, then you can dig into that. If it's the stuff all over the place in the family room, what is that stuff specifically? Maybe all the stuff shows you that your kids are busily and happily playing and exploring: they are learning. Can you walk into the room and see the learning instead of the mess? If the main play room is the first thing you see when you walk into the house and it knocks you off your game immediately, can you maybe move the main play area somewhere else? A more out-of-the-way and rarely used dining room? The basement? Can you think of a way to make your children an awesome play space that will also keep the messes less conspicuous?

Can the current play space be reorganized so that it's much easier for you to quickly tidy up? A wall of shelving or a set of plastic bins that makes tidying up easier, and maybe a bit more enjoyable. And don't forget to look at things from your children's perspectives too: would they be okay with you tidying up their stuff? Maybe what you see as messes is really a wonderful work in progress in their imagination and your "tidying" is more like "destroying" in their eyes (which would interfere with their learning). Ask them. Play with them and see how and when the messes grow. More information for you. If they are okay with you tidying up and you do so, are they excited to see a clean play space, a fresh canvas? They are learning about their environment. And you have given them a beautiful gift in that moment.

When you understand more about their needs surrounding play and works in progress and a fresh play space, and your real needs for some semblance of tidy in some area(s), it's a great time to ask everyone for help—work together as a family to brainstorm ideas and figure out a path forward that works for everyone without having to resorting to control through assigned chores. In my experience, when I'm tempted to reach for control or coercion as a tool, it usually means that I haven't taken the time to understand the other person's point of view (because if I had, I'd understand why they didn't want to do it in the first place) or I am trying to get them to take care of my needs (it's something I want, but I don't want to do the work myself to get there).

As you talk with your family here and there about your needs (the real ones, the ones that go deeper than "keep the house clean," which to them would seem a vague and gargantuan task) remember, you're not trying to come up with expectations that you'll hold them to. Show, don't tell. If you guys decide to add shelving and bins to make tidying up easier, you've made it easier for those who want to tidy up to do so. Maybe that's just you and your partner right now. And a tip: don't be grumpy about it! Who would want to join in, or initiate, an activity that makes people grumpy and/or that others seem to avoid as long as possible?

"There are a lot of toys on the floor and I'm finding it distracting. Are you guys finished playing with these stuffed animals over here? Is it okay if I put them back in their box?" Lead by example: let them see you taking care of *your* needs. With that perspective and attitude, they won't develop a sense of entitlement, an expectation that you'll do everything for them, because they'll know you're *not* doing it for them, you're doing it for you.

And sometime, maybe later when it's no longer a charged issue, you'll enjoy surprising them with a clean slate. Or they may excitedly ask you to do it, or to help them. They'll see you as choosing to do it, not as you fulfilling an expectation of theirs. You're helping them discover the joy of a tidy space. Which, if they do find it enjoyable, will naturally motivate them at some point to do it for themselves, to meet their *own* needs. Real learning.

And in my experience, once the topic is no longer a battleground, they'll happily choose to help you out when they can too. Living and learning together.

How Do Unschooling Children
Learn How to Act in Society?

Reader Question:

I recently interacted with a family with 3 children who are following unschooling principles. The biggest concern I see is the lack of discipline; and that children are not taught manners necessary to act in socially-acceptable ways in others' homes. How do unschooled children learn manners so they know how to act in society?

I read your books on unschooling, so I think I know what this mother is trying to accomplish. However, she seems to be adopting a "laissez-faire" approach—giving the children carte blanche to act and do whatever comes to mind, with no boundaries, and no guidance, and then using I-messages in an attempt to understand the frustrating situations the child finds himself in.

In your book "Free to Live," you state "Patience doesn't mean carte blanche" and you give the example of a boy's rude behavior in the playground. You state that parents new to unschooling might misunderstand the principles of unschooling, and believe they should give their children free rein to do whatever they please, whenever they feel like it. I wish and hope you'd go on to explain how to avoid this pitfall.

*****

Let's start here:

You state that parents new to unschooling might misunderstand the principles of unschooling, and believe they should give their children free rein to do whatever they please, whenever they feel like it. I wish and hope you'd go on to explain how to avoid this pitfall.

When people first start learning about unschooling it does sometimes happen that, as they look to stop controlling their children, they overcompensate and swing too far in the opposite direction. In an effort to avoid imposing their will, they end up giving their children little feedback or support about the environments in which they find themselves. They are still seeing their relationships from the perspective of "power," and in trying to give their children more power, they almost completely remove themselves from the equation of any given situation.

It's important to note that this may just be a step in their journey, part of their exploration of what parenting looks like within the context of unschooling. As they continue to learn about unschooling and observe their children's behaviour in various contexts, many discover that disconnect and begin to work more effectively *with* their children, more actively supporting them as they explore and interact with the world at large.

How might you help them see these other possibilities?

If they're receptive, as you and your children interact, you might conversationally share a sentence or two about why you chose to do or say something. As situations arise, share what you've done in similar circumstances. Make it about *your* parenting, not theirs. Share bits and pieces of your experiences and let them make the connections that make sense for them. That is where real learning lies. You can also encourage them to continue learning about unschooling: more bits and pieces to connect to their growing understanding. Just remember that you can't control their learning—in the end, it's their journey to take.

... and then using I-messages in an attempt to understand the frustrating situations the child finds himself in.

I wanted to talk about this for a moment. I understand the idea behind using I-messages as a tool to help parents move away from using controlling language to manipulate their children's behaviour. But sometimes I-messages, which encourage us to observe situations from our own perspective and then share that information, can get in the way of seeing things through our children's eyes. We stop at our perspective.

In my experience, when I stop filtering things through my point of view and shift to seeing things from my children's perspective, I gain a much deeper appreciation of what they are trying to accomplish. And from *that* place of greater understanding, I can add in my understanding of the other people involved and of the world in general, and share the pieces of the bigger perspective that will help my children the most. Not just how I'm seeing the situation, but also validating how it looks to them, sharing how Grandma sees it, and how they all mesh together. Then I can share my ideas on how we might *all* get our needs met, and discussion can open up and flow from there.

How do unschooled children learn manners so they know how to act in society?

Unschooling parents actively help their children understand the ins and outs of social situations. It's about understanding your children individually. Chat with them beforehand about what will be expected of them in the situation, and why. Are they comfortable with it? Can they handle it? Not do you think they *should* be able to do it, but are they capable? And are they willing? If they don't understand or won't likely remember what is expected in a social situation, and if they and/or the parents still want to go, then it will behoove the parents to stay close to their children and actively help them as things arise. And to actively advocate for them where they think some leeway is appropriate.

I'll give you an example from when my kids were young and we'd visit my husband's family for Sunday lunch. I'd do what I could to set it up for success. First, I'd chat with my hubby to understand the ins and outs of the expectations. Then I'd talk with my kids beforehand about them, in a conversational way, not in a "you need to do this" kind of way. Because when they weren't able and/or willing, I'd always step up to help.

For example, on arrival, it was expected that they kids would seek out and say hi to the older relatives—grandparents, etc. That's a pretty socially polite thing to do. But when my kids were younger, understandably that wasn't something that interested them. I'd mention it at home when we chatted about visiting, explaining the reason behind it: they were excited the grandkids had arrived and wanted a moment to greet them. But on any particular visit, if any of my children felt intimidated or out of sorts, I'd happily pick them up and do the talking—both protecting them, and satisfying extended family. They didn't need to be actively participating to see these social practices playing out. They didn't need to be "forced" to take part in them when they were uncomfortable to learn them. They took them over when they were ready—it was a pretty seamless process.

Some other ways I helped them navigate the ins and outs of the occasion? I'd bring toys, and play *with* them, to keep the kids engaged so they enjoyed the time. I'd keep an eye on the lunch prep and let the kids know when it was getting close and that we'd be going to sit at the table to eat. I'd dish up their plates and prep their food so it was easy for them to eat, minimizing frustration at the table. When they were done eating and leaving the table, *I* would excuse them, asking them if they were full and so on. That way the other adults would know they had my okay to leave (as well as having heard my reason: they were full). Then any frustration the other adults had would be directed at me, not the kids. I was the buffer. And exuding confidence and joy throughout the visit also went a long way.

As an unschooling parent I want to help my children explore the world, including any social situations they may find themselves in. Just remember, there are not a lot of things we truly "have to" do. But if we *want* to do them, it's worth the effort to make them as enjoyable as possible without negatively impacting those around them— because, everything being equal, the children don't want that either. To figure all that out, they need real information. And someone to bounce it all around with. It takes time and effort, but not only does it help them enjoy the moment, it's how they gain experience analyzing situations and choosing ways to move through them that they feel good about.

And last, but not least, for those learning about unschooling who may find themselves veering more into hands-off parenting rather than active support, I thought I'd snapshot a couple of situations I've seen mentioned lately and share some ideas on how to approach them.

During social visits, children are offered candy and then leave a mess behind them.

Knowing my young children would enjoy the candy but that it's often a messy affair, and that my hosts wouldn't appreciate extra cleaning, I'd find a way for both things to happen. When the offer was made I'd probably invite them outside, "Those look delicious! Why don't we enjoy them outside so we don't make a mess in the house?" The problem and the solution all in one short sentence. Notice I don't *send* them outside, I go with them.

If they aren't interested in that, maybe I'd offer up a game to play at the kitchen table (like a dice game—something plastic that I could easily wash up when we were done, or a verbal game like twenty questions). Or to watch a short video, sitting on the floor, maybe putting down a plastic tablecloth and going picnic-style, to minimize the mess. At a minimum I'd stay with them and tidy up any pieces of candy that dropped, "Oops, let me put in the garbage so we don't make a mess." Again, short and sweet. I'd probably grab a bag to have with me, and it may well become a game, them putting what they're done with in the bag.

There are many possibilities that would keep everyone happy.

A child is inconsolable when something doesn't unfold as expected and the parent works to recreate the situation to match what their child envisioned.

Often people who see this unfold are concerned it will teach the child that every situation should go as they want and that they aren't learning how to deal with "real life." The short answer is no, it won't—unless that's the motivation with which the mother is approaching it. I remember doing that with my children sometimes. It does *not* mean they'll need to process things this way for the rest of their life. That's more projection and fear talking.

Sometimes when reality doesn't unfold the way the child is expecting, it's profoundly disappointing. And sometimes a re-enactment can help them process it all. It may seem to an outsider that all that is happening is they "get their way," but it can be a helpful part of the process of learning about themselves. Now they have two memories/experiences to call upon: one where things went the way they were expected, and one where they didn't—a do-over doesn't erase the initial experience.

But, don't expect or insist others to participate. Absolutely some might be willing to help out, but in those moments *I* was the one trying to help my child explore ways to process the experience at hand; it wasn't anyone else's responsibility.

What about College?

If you've been unschooling your children for any length of time, you've likely been asked this question. And it's a good one! During our lifetime, a college degree has been practically synonymous with getting a good job and being conventionally successful. It's no wonder that family and friends worry that our unconventional path may force our children to forfeit the golden egg.

And certainly we can debate the value of the conventional definition of "success," but today let's focus on the learning side of the college coin. In what ways can unschooling teens and young adults continue to learn? When is college a useful destination?

To this point much of humanity's body of knowledge has been ensconced in colleges and universities, making it the "go to" place to expand your horizons, but over the last few decades we have been witness to an incredible transition. The explosion of information, the growth of technology, and the resultant blossoming of near real-time communication between people around the globe has created an entirely new backdrop to our lives.

Society is really just beginning to embrace this exponential increase in connectedness, to wrap its head around the implications and contemplate what might be possible. A number of interesting online learning communities have been created over the last few years and they are growing and changing constantly.

For example, more and more free learning resources have been made available online, a smattering of which includes: iTunes, Khan Academy, MIT's OpenCourse-Ware, and edX (founded by Harvard and MIT and offering free courses from many universities around the world). These are wonderful resources to have access to! They are a first step in rethinking how we might support learning in this new, highly-connected world and there are definite advantages beyond the free access: the learner is more in control of both the content (they can skip around the course material) and the pace (they can move through the material at the speed that best suits them). Yet still, the focus is on bringing the typical teacher-student, curriculum-driven, learning paradigm into the online space.

Moving a step closer to a bigger-picture view of learning, TED Talks expand beyond academic topics and focus on sharing ideas for discussion and engagement, connecting interested learners with those passionate about their topic. And TED curators have created great tools, like play lists and tags, to slice and dice the data and narrow in on those ideas that speak to you.

I do love that this growth of information access seems likely to shift control of the learning process from the conventional teacher to the learner, something unschooling parents see as a key ingredient in learning. And, in tandem, I think it will help people shift their focus and see the *learning*, not just the degree. How? With more people participating in these less formal courses and learning communities, they will start showing up regularly in discussions and on resumés. We'll see more and more people with solid knowledge and skills to use and share, gained without jumping through the typical college degree hoop. Businesses will *want* to find and hire them, just as colleges and universities are discovering the unique skills of homeschooled students and creating homeschooling admission policies.

Another interesting slice of the online world is focusing on all the many other ways to learn beyond college. There's Dale Stephen's UnCollege. From the website: "UnCollege is a social movement designed to help you hack your education. This manifesto will show you how to gain the passion, hustle, and contrarianism requisite for success — all without setting foot inside a classroom." Granted, his target audience seems to be typical students that are looking for alternatives to the conventional college path. Experienced unschoolers likely already possess the curiosity, confidence, and grit he speaks of, yet they too may find inspiration through the blog and/or Dale's book, *Hacking Your Education*, plus various in-person events.

For experienced unschoolers looking for like-minded community there's Blake Boles' Zero Tuition College, an "online community of self-directed learners who educate themselves without college." There you can connect with others, including a mentoring aspect. Blake's book, *Better Than College: How to Build a Successful Life Without a Four-Year Degree*, has been well-received.

Or maybe your teen or young adult isn't interested in connecting around lifestyle but is instead interested in connecting around shared interests and passions, a main-stay of unschooling. That's great too! People love to share their passions with others, and the internet has made gathering around interests so easy to do. Pick *any* interest and I'm sure you'll find others who share it through blogs or mailing lists or forums; through Twitter or Tumblr or Facebook groups or Google+ circles or whatever the social media of choice. People are amazing! Not only have I learned so much about unschooling over the years, I've also learned incredible amounts about writing, self-publishing, online businesses, food and cooking, video games, movies and TV shows and actors, and books by my favourite authors ... so many things. The web is a fantastical tool!

So what might contemplating this "what about col-lege" question look like in real life? I thought I'd share a snapshot of what it has looked like for my daughter at nineteen as an example. Probably starting in earnest around age fifteen, Lissy, who had developed a deep love for photography, began exploring the possibilities for ex-panding her passion. Alongside her everyday exploration of photography, over the next couple of years she re-viewed college curricula for photography programs at in-stitutions near and far, spoke with people in some of those programs and in the industry at large, and researched the beginning journeys of established photographers. This wasn't a case of "you're approaching college age so you better figure out what your next step is" but of "I've been immersing myself in my passion for a few years now and I want to connect with others as passionate as I am and expand my learning." Note the perspective—the impetus was coming from her.

From this searching and contemplation a path forward that seemed to best mesh with her goals began to emerge and at age eighteen she chose to spend six months living in and exploring New York City to see if it met her wish for community and learning. For her, it was stellar! It fed her soul in so many of the ways she was looking for. From there we spent countless hours over a couple of months gathering evidence and letters and all the other minutiae that make up a US artist's visa application. During that time, in conversation with our more conventional family and friends, we likened the lawyer's fees to college tuition—that seemed to help them make the connection that this was in support of real learning in the world. Her application was approved for the full three years and she moved there. In the last year her knowledge and understanding of photography and the business world that surrounds it has grown exponentially!

Yet none of this means that college is forever out of the picture. Maybe her interests will change—one of the keys to finding joy in life is to not to feel locked into anything, to remember that whatever you do, it's always a choice. Maybe she will encounter a program, or even just a course, that intersects with something she is looking to learn.

I think what's important for teens, and parents, is to see college as a tool that can be used to meet a goal; not as a goal in and of itself. College is an option on the learning platter. It seems much less useful, and more expensive, to go to college to "figure out what you want to do in life." Instead, when you figure out what you'd like to pursue, if there's interesting and unique knowledge and/or community available at college, *that's* when it merits serious consideration.

And if that moment comes, depending on the program, maybe your teen will need to spend some time picking up some prerequisite classes. Maybe online, or in a remedial class or two to pick up some of the skills needed (likely alongside students who did go to school and still didn't pick them up). Maybe they'll start at another college with minimal entrance requirements to build a student record and then transfer to the college and program of their choice. None of that means unschooling failed. Unschooling teens haven't been doing nothing—they were busy learning *other* things. Just because they weren't things that could be used to check off these particular requirement boxes, doesn't mean it was time wasted. With a lifelong view of learning there is no ahead or behind, there is stuff you know and stuff you want to learn. Regardless of age. It's life.

CHAPTER NINE

:: perspective ::

Some of the ways my perspective on things has grown through unschooling.

Unschooling Grows Far beyond "Not School"

It's pretty typical to move through adulthood staying generally disengaged from life: you get a job, get married, have kids, send them to school. It's quite easy to do—the conventional treadmill carries you along and delivers you to each stop without much effort of your part. Yet for many, there's an inner conflict between what lives in their heart and the societal expectations in their head. Many manage to ignore it until midlife when, as children move out and things slow down, they find themselves evaluating their life so far and get tangled up in the aptly named mid-life crisis.

Others are drawn to examine the disconnect earlier, often following the hearts and minds of their children. No matter the path that led you to unschooling, with it you are choosing to step off the conventional treadmill. And once you've taken that first step it becomes harder and harder to continue down that well-worn path of conven-tion—unschooling soon asks us to examine the deeper questions.

When we choose unschooling we often do so with the intention of opening up the possibilities for our chil-dren, of giving them the space and the support to forge their own path through childhood. Yet as we watch them in action, often spellbound, our minds begin to stretch further and soon we start asking that of ourselves. As unschooling parents we espouse the joy of learning, champion the idea of lifelong learning ... and we begin to realize that it applies to us as well. Our perspective grows. Who am I? What is *my* path? What kind of parent do I want to be? It becomes apparent that even as adults we are not "done"; we can learn and change and take small steps each day towards being the person we want to become.

We see our children exploring life with zeal. They are enthusiastically vocal in celebration of even the small-est victories, and in the next moment are struggling with frustration and deep sadness as things go awry—each ex-perience is expressed from the depths of their soul. We begin to reawaken, to remember what it means to be so directly engaged with life. It is beautiful! And we begin to feel protective of our children, not wanting them to lose that openness, that depth of feeling, both joy and sorrow, as they get older. It begins to dawn on us that if we so eagerly want them to retain that lust for life into adulthood, if that's what living can look like in all its glory, as adults, couldn't we be living that too? Yes!

With that realization we are drawn to exploring ourselves, to finding that depth of engagement in life, with all its twists and turns and ups and downs. For maybe the first time we really see the value in nurturing our spirit. It stuns us. We marvel that the journey we started to fully and deeply support our children and their learning has turned so completely around and *we* are learning so much from *them* about being alive and fully engaged with life. We probably didn't even realize we were encased in a layer of conventional goo, a dour mix of expectations and judgment and fear, until we managed to wipe some away and rediscover that the world is fresh and interesting and inspiring!

We are always learning. The learning is *in* the living. Looking back, I realize the biggest gift we give to our children and ourselves with unschooling is *time*. Time to live and to learn and to do it all again the next day, the next week, the next month. Time to cocoon, time to process, time to reflect. Time is at our disposal; it is not our master.

When you first begin unschooling it can feel like such a huge leap—one day the kids are going to school and the next day they aren't. Or they hit school age and the first day of school comes and they don't go. It *is* huge! And faced with that momentous act, it's so easy to get caught up in the idea that it must be met with equally huge goals and plans and activities. Instead, try baby steps. Gradual, yet determined, steps towards the person you want to be. And remember to take time for reflection, for turning your thoughts and observations over in your mind, for playing with the puzzle pieces and seeing how they fit together. It is in this time of contemplation that so many connections fall into place. And don't fret that you need swaths of alone sitting time to think—I recall many aha moments while doing the dishes, or in the shower, or tidying up the toys.

What else do we discover? That no matter how strongly we wish to know and understand it all *right now*, to have this life thing figured out—what makes us tick, what brings a smile to our face, and why fear sometimes trickles in—it is a process, a cycle. Round and round and round. As a parent, as a person, you never reach the end of learning because with each iteration through another question or challenge your children are older and more experienced, and you are older and more experienced. New things are coming into your lives and others are dropping out, all of which bring new insights. There's *always* more to learn and understand—about ourselves, about others, about the world.

And somewhere along the line it dawned on me that it's not about figuring it all out so I can *finally*, from that moment on, live a happy life. This process *is* a well-lived life.

A Positive Outlook Isn't
Turning a Blind Eye

Living joyfully with unschooling doesn't mean that life no longer has disappointments or challenges, so let's talk a bit about when things go wrong. You know, those moments when maybe you act or react without thinking, or when things seem to go from bad to worse and worse again.

One tip I've found helpful over the years, which I believe I first heard from Sandra Dodd: remember these are just moments, don't be tempted to paint your whole day as a "bad day." Each new moment is a chance to do something differently. If you stay in that place of disappointment or frustration it colours your perspective as you move through the rest of your day: you view, act, and react through that filter. All of a sudden a handful of things not going perfectly becomes the world out to get you. (Note: the world isn't out to get you.) So there's a really good reason to take the time to put the frustrating moments into perspective and move forward fresh. Your next moments aren't tainted before they even happen.

I've tried all sorts of ways over the years to make that shift—you'll discover it depends on the circumstances and the people involved. Play around and see what works for you and your family. I recall some mornings that were going off the rails because I seemed to be doing all the wrong things, trying to direct things more than the kids were comfortable with. Sometimes I would try to break the tension by joking about going back to bed to start over. I'm pretty sure we actually did it a couple times. We closed our eyes and pretended to sleep for a minute, then rolled over and yawned, saying good morning. And from there I'd consciously slow down and watch my kids more closely for clues, being careful to follow *them* this time, to be patient and see what was in their minds that seemed to be at odds with my approach that morning. Over the years, mounting frustration on my part has become a clue that it's probably time to shift my focus away from myself.

What also helps me is to give just as much weight, if not more, to the good moments, or else the challenging moments seem to get all my attention, and fill my memories. The good moments certainly don't need to be big and fancy ... a couple nights ago I was picking up my son Michael at his dojo, and we ended up hanging around outside after class, chatting with a handful of the teens. The conversation eventually ebbed and I went to the car, thinking we'd be leaving, but a new topic must have reared its head because he didn't follow, so I spent the next five minutes just watching them from the car. It was beautiful: chatter and smiles and laughter and hugs and spins. I took a mental picture, and spent a moment appreciating the people we have in our lives.

I could have been all, "Michael, we have to leave, I have groceries in the car and the ice cream is melting!" The thought crossed my mind, but which would have the most impact in the bigger picture: ice cream safe in the freezer or deepening friendships? In that moment fond memories were being created, strengthening his connections with the dojo and with his friends, learning more about their lives and their thoughts and laughing at their jokes. It's not just the big, expectation-laden moments that help us figure out who we are and who we want to be—it's in these small moments of flow and almost effortless connection where we find so much of ourselves. I've come to realize that noticing and appreciating these everyday moments is so helpful in living joyfully. And that habit grew out of taking the time when we first came to unschooling to notice and appreciate the many small moments of learning in my children's lives.

And another, at first seemingly unrelated, piece of the moments puzzle. Learning about unschooling, thinking about the principles behind it, has helped me realize the importance of understanding myself. How could I ask myself to create a solid unschooling environment for my children if I didn't understand myself well enough to make the day-to-day choices that better serve that longer-term goal?

One thing that grew out of that line of questioning was a deeper understanding of how I can make better choices. Turns out, a big part of that for me is having a positive outlook. In my extended family I'm kinda known for having a positive outlook—it's a choice that I make. It's not that I'm ignoring the challenges, turning a blind eye, but that I know I do my best thinking in a positive mindset.

When I'm doused in fear, my mind circles round and round and round—I can barely string three thoughts together, let alone make reasonable choices. When I have enough presence of mind to recognize that it's happening,

I am patient with myself as I move through it, not demanding myself to make quick decisions. I take the time I need to move through the fear reaction, to let the adrenaline surge fade a bit, to let my breathing get back to normal. Even with life-altering challenges, most often there is time for that. Not many are in-the-moment emergencies.

A positive outlook through challenges isn't about convincing myself that the problem is really a blessing in disguise (though I don't rule that out either—sometimes my mind just hasn't caught up to reality yet). It's about moving through the initial fear to a place where I see the other side. I may not know what it looks like, or how I'm going to get there, but I see a point in the distance to shoot for—I have shifted my perspective to the bigger picture.

From there my brain begins to unfreeze. And with that positive outlook, when everything is no longer clouded in shadow, I can see situations so much more clearly. I can start brainstorming and asking questions and thinking through possibilities. I can better analyze situations. And often I see that I don't have to actually make a decision right now, that I have time to take a step and see where it leads. And then another step, and another, gathering information and experience, which help me to eventually discover my path forward.

A bigger perspective. An understanding that life's challenges aren't my fault, nor is the world ganging up on me (if you find your challenges are consistently the result of your actions, it's time for a different conversation with yourself). In that mindset, my brain works so much more effectively to explore the possibilities for moving through it. And with each experience of moving through a challenge, that deeper sense of capability, of personal power, of joy, grows.

My unschooling journey has brought so much more to my life than I first imagined it could.

A Lifetime of Living and Learning

Looking back over our years of unschooling, it's become clear that my perspective as a parent has broadened beyond "childhood" to "life." I no longer see childhood as focused on "learning everything you need to know to become an adult."

I think this shift started when I began pondering the purpose of curriculum, actually. From asking myself many questions about why children "should" learn certain things at certain ages. From thinking about what I learned at school, the messages I was given about learning, and my own experience with what I have found truly useful as an adult.

Some of the thoughts that bubbled up along the way:

- there isn't a discrete set of knowledge and skills that everyone *must* have;
- the discrete set of knowledge and skills that is helpful for people to interact comfortably with their own communities, varies by community (both cultural communities and those gathered

around interests), and includes a subset of the typical school curriculum and much beyond it;

- without the overlay of others' expectations, children *want* to participate in the world around them as much as they are able, and the motivation to learn the knowledge and skills to do so grows organically alongside: to the level that they want to participate in the world around them, they want to do so successfully (as judged by themselves); which leads us to

- any piece of knowledge or skill worth having is worth learning when that value is discovered—and bonus, that knowledge or skill is better understood, and often more easily learned, at that time, i.e., when the learner has discovered a need for it, when they have discovered a missing piece in their puzzle of the world, and they want to fill it (great internal motivation); and

- giving everyone a generalized and basic picture of the world sounds good when looking from a 10,000 foot level at society in general, but it doesn't translate well down to the individual—the individual has their own unique life to live and much of that general information may not be relevant or useful to them.

It's so easy to tell ourselves that there's no real harm in insisting a child learn something that's not useful to them. It can't hurt, right? Well first off, they'll probably forget it soon after, so it's not really learned. Not to mention that their time is wasted and could be put to better use learning things that interests them and are useful to them today. But what they pick up long-term through the endless repetition of "learn this, you'll need to know it someday," can be harmful: they learn to not trust themselves, to not trust their own judgment. They learn that others know better than they do what's important for them. They learn to be followers; they feel safer looking for someone else to tell them what they "should" know, to tell them what the "right" thing to do is, rather than thinking for themselves.

That seems like quite a bit of harm being done in the name of "someday." Why can't they learn "it," whatever it is, when "someday" actually comes? *If* it ever comes (and if it doesn't, then they never did encounter a use for it). They can. If you don't ingrain in them the idea that they need to learn "everything" in childhood in order to "graduate" into adulthood, they will be open to learning new things whenever the interest or need arises, whatever their age. Keeping my frame of reference for learning firmly focused on "lifetime" rather than "childhood" has helped my children develop an approach to learning that will be useful to them both today and throughout their lifetime.

Over the years this perspective has been so helpful, time and again. I see the learning my young adult children are continuing to do. I see the learning *I* am continuing to do. Our learning is better understood and remembered when we're actively pursuing the information or skill: when we're interested. And we have a lifetime to learn things.

Childhood is not preparation for life; it's an integral part of it.

Treasure Creativity

Since we began unschooling, my appreciation for creativity has grown immeasurably. When we first started out, I thought creativity was great for artists, yet not particularly useful beyond that. But over the years I came to see how valuable it is to have a creative approach to life, and that unschooling is a wonderful way to help children retain their creativity. I think children are naturally creative, but that many of our conventional parenting and teaching practices discourage its use.

Let's look at creativity from some different perspectives.

Creative Arts

We'll start with the obvious visual and performance arts. With the conventional focus in childhood on right and wrong, and even more so in schools as teachers grade their work, judgment often funnels young artists into the "box." The adult reactions to blue trees, dissonant chords, and new dance moves often send young artists the message that their imagination should stay firmly within the bounds of reality and convention.

One of my daughter's favourite quotes is from Walt Disney, "Every child is born blessed with a vivid imagination. But just as a muscle grows flabby with disuse, the bright imagination of a child pales in later years if he ceases to exercise it."

With unschooling, a child is free, and even better, encouraged, to follow their own path of engagement with the creative arts. And that can be a very individual dance, especially if they are passionately drawn to an art form. At times they may be exploring the techniques, experiences, and ideas of other artists, both directly in their field of interest and beyond. And at other times they may be pulling inward, connecting those thoughts to their own understanding, letting their imagination percolate and play. Unschooling parents are partners in this dance, sharing their thoughts and perspective, while being careful not to fall into judgment, artificially restricting their child's playground—their imagination.

Analyzing Situations and Creative Solutions

A yes/no answer, followed up with "because I said so," is often the quickest way to move on in the moment, but there isn't much learning or creative thinking happening there. One of the things that makes unschooling more time consuming is that rather than perpetuating the black and white distinction of right/wrong, we spend time looking at situations from various angles. In many everyday moments there are other possible paths to take beyond the "yes to one person, no the other" path. It's possible that the needs of everyone involved can be accommodated—it just might take some creative thinking to figure out how.

Analyzing situations is about finding the real parameters and exploring the needs of the people involved. From there, our minds can dance through the possibilities. Paths don't need to be as the crow flies—sometimes efficiency isn't the most important goal. That's where thinking outside the box shines!

Sometimes I'm a bit stunned by how little creativity many adults put into their thinking. When a question or issue arises, they think of the typical answer and stop there. Anything outside the conventional has too much risk associated with it—they have thoroughly learned to crave the comfort of the box. They can't see the possibilities a bit further down the path, the tangible opportunities that may grow out of an unconventional experience.

Imagine how useful these skills will be in adulthood! Being able to analyze situations and think creatively will help them in many ways, from discovering obscure yet rewarding paths to meet their own goals, to working with team members and finding unique ways to meet their company's business goals, to exploring the possibilities of life with their own children. Are you finding your journey to unschooling is flexing your creative thinking muscles?

Creative Learning

I am still amazed at how rich and fulfilling learning is off the conventional path. When I started my unschooling journey, I was just beginning to glimpse the learning that can happen outside the school system. Over the years, that glimpse has blossomed into a rich and diverse landscape. Unschoolers explore the world through their interests and passions, reaching out and connecting and learning and growing. This real learning is understood and remembered, it's appreciated and enjoyed, and most often it's fun! And it's all around us.

That doesn't mean it's "easy." Life is full of challenges. Yet unschooling helps young people discover the things they are so interested in that setbacks, even though disappointing, aren't major deterrents that knock them off their path. Instead, they are pieces of information that can be used to tweak their course. With unschoolers, their internal motivation is often captivating.

Over the years I've seen unschoolers take so many different paths to learning things, to finding a place in the adult world. As unschooling teens dig into their interests and passions, they find communities and make connections, whether face-to-face or online. Even when they dip into more conventional learning tools, like college, they come at it from an entirely different perspective because they are there by *choice*. They want to *learn*, not just get a degree. Not only do their unique learning experiences and passion for their field come across in their resume, but in my experience, their excitement for their field of interest often means they are sought after by others as passionate as they are. Watching unschoolers move into the adult world is so interesting!

I have come to treasure the creativity that unschooling nurtures. Giving the priority, space, and time to culti-

vate the perspective of being open-minded and seeing possibilities, of thinking for themselves and seeing what happens, allows life to play out in marvelous ways time and
again.

What Makes a Successful Life?

We started unschooling in 2002, and looking back, one of
the biggest changes in my worldview has been my definition of "success." It's so much bigger now. Moving to
unschooling really challenged me to re-evaluate my life
goals, both my personal ones and my parenting ones.

Success is one of those words with layers. On the surface it's about reaching our goals—certainly we'd all like to
accomplish the things we set out to do. Yet underneath, it
implies the attainment of wealth and social position. And
deeper still, that the only goals worth actively pursuing are
ones that result in one (or better, both) of those outcomes.
When we buy into that perspective of success, it means
that we quickly discard goals that don't hold the promise
of wealth at the end.

I grew up learning all the conventional, at least in
North America, markers of success: a large home, fancy
cars, name brand clothing, and sunny vacations. And
though it's slowly changing, my experience is that this is
still the dominant perspective. So for many, chasing success means choosing and accomplishing goals that result in
the highest earnings attainable, which in turn allows them

to purchase (sometimes through debt, against future antic-ipated earnings) those symbols of success. Certainly, some personal satisfaction is gained as those luxurious items meet, and often exceed, their needs, but I think there is also the satisfaction of showing others that they have "won"—competition is a significant part of the picture.

And school is all tied up in this conventional path to success: finding jobs with high earning potential typically means jobs that require additional schooling, i.e., a college or university degree. And getting into college means a high school diploma, with high marks as students compete to get in. Of course, doing well in high school means spending grade school mastering the educational system, i.e., getting good at taking tests. I bought that story. I *lived* that story.

But having children, and later considering unschooling, led me to question the repercussions of that path. I began to deeply wonder, does achieving conven-tional success lead to happiness? Because it didn't take me long to realize that enjoying one's time on this planet is definitely a worthwhile goal. That soon led me to distin-guish between the fleeting happiness (distraction?) of be-ing able to purchase new things and live very comfortably (is there meaning to life beyond being physically comfort-able?) that would need to be continually fed (when is enough, enough?), and a more soulful contentment with one's direction in life. A feeling of meaningful accom-plishment, of having a positive impact on those around you. A sense of satisfaction that runs deeper than the ups and downs of day-to-day happenings.

Pondering that further, I came to see that rather than choosing goals specifically for their potential monetary success, it was more important that the goals a person is successfully accomplishing has meaning *for them.* And while the school path may more directly lead into pursuing conventional success, the unschooling path encompasses the learning, both about themselves and the world, and encourages the mindset that leads to the pursuit of more personally fulfilling goals. How? With unschooling, the focus is on doing things that interest them, that bring them joy. On accomplishments that are much more likely to bring them personal satisfaction and a sense of meaningful achievement. Over and over.

Neither course precludes the other: I took the conventional path and here I am, living a decidedly unconventional life. And an unschooling childhood by no means prohibits one from achieving conventional-looking success (though it will probably be done from a completely different perspective, simultaneously fulfilling their personal goals), regardless of how often fear motivates strangers and relatives alike to proclaim that your unschooling children are doomed to work low-paying service jobs forever. (And I had a hard time writing that because there's nothing inherently wrong with choosing to work those jobs either, but you get my point.)

For me, it's come to be about personal choices. Maybe someone is choosing a larger home because it gives the family room to spread out, space to pursue their projects, to find some needed privacy—those are all valuable, personal, meaningful reasons. Same with choosing a smaller home—it's about the individuals involved. Same for fancy cars. Maybe it's their passion, maybe they love restoration, maybe it's about the high performance, or maybe it's about design. I've learned not to judge others' choices just because they aren't the same as mine. Because they *aren't* mine. I'm not inside their heads, their thoughts and feelings and history, whatever brought them to this moment in their lives.

Instead of placing societal expectations above their own desires, unschooled young adults are making choices—work, career, jobs, hobbies, etc.—based on their *own* interests and needs, which, through unschooling, they have gained lots of experience doing. Their goals are an amalgamation of their interests and dreams and personality and passions and circumstances. Life is about being successful at whatever they choose to pursue, rather than pursuing success in and of itself.

Pursuing success for its own sake is more often a hollow victory because it has no deeper meaning for the individual than the reward. Satisfaction is short-lived and you're back on the treadmill, needing another hit. It is the essence of external motivation, looking outside yourself for something to meet your need to feel successful. Whereas when you love what you're doing, when you enjoy the work *as well as* the result, you discover a deep well of internal motivation. Deep and lasting satisfaction lives there. In that world, most days feel successful.

It's so easy to dismiss the advice to find work that you truly enjoy, love even, as unrealistic. Most people don't enjoy their job. Conventional school has trained most people to believe that work—and school is presented as work for children—is not fun. That's what weekends are for. Even in the dictionary, work and fun are antonyms—opposites.

But with unschooling, we choose our activities and actively pursue things we enjoy, in other words, we regularly have fun. And I've come to realize that in doing this not only do we learn better, we also *perform* better. Learning or doing, we find ourselves immersed "in the flow" of the activity more often.

When an opportunity presents itself, it really is okay, valuable even, to ask yourself if you think it will be fun to do. When it's fun, you will enjoy it. You will, without feeling put upon or taken advantage of, put more effort into it. And when it feels like play, your mind will relax, open up, and slip into the flow, giving you more opportunity to make new and interesting connections: whether it's a piece of art, a chunk of programming, or a business proposal. When it's fun, there's a *better* chance of spectacular results. Of success.

Mindfulness and Unschooling

I love the variety of words that express the concept of being mindful: observant, aware, attentive, conscientious, careful, cognizant, considerate, present, respectful, thoughtful, sensible.

Living mindfully is a skill that I picked up as I played with creating a solid unschooling environment in our home. Being mindful walks hand in hand with unschooling because they both call us to be observant and make conscious choices, see how they play out, and incorporate those experiences into our lives moving forward. It's how we learn, regardless of age—from learning to walk to figuring out games to discerning our sleep patterns to improving our communication skills to choosing our work. So much of unschooling is about being aware of our environment, ourselves, the people in our lives, and the ways they all swirl together.

Unschooling asks us to become more aware of our filters so we might notice more quickly when they are clouding our vision. This also helps us see situations more clearly from our children's perspective and better understand their actions and reactions. When we meet them where they are, we can more effectively support them as they explore and learn about the world.

Being attentive to the present moment helps us see not only the bigger actions playing out in front of us, but the smaller ones too. A fleeting smile of understanding on our child's face. A quick tensing of our partner's shoulders. A short burst of giggles from a nearby room. A momentary feeling of unease as our child attempts something for the first time. These are subtle yet important clues about our experiences. They don't necessarily demand any action on our part, but we'll do well to add them to our collection of observations, small puzzle pieces that may one day become part of the bigger picture of our understanding of ourselves, our children, and our world.

Being alert and mindful also helps us catch the good moments, the ones that might rush past our consciousness without acknowledgment because they don't have a direct impact on us. A child sharing a toy with their sibling, or comforting a playmate at the park. Our spouse filling up the gas tank, or playing a game with the kids. All the small moments of caring and connection that populate our days. It's so easy to miss those moments, or dismiss them. Yet they mean so much in the bigger picture—our world is full of small acts of kindness.

Something else I've learned from being mindful of my thoughts and actions is to give space for being wrong. For me, being in the moment has shown me that I cannot predict the future with any significant sense of certainty. Giving up my expectations of the next moment has meant I don't leap so quickly into moments to try to "fix" or direct them—with my kids, or with other adults. Through giving those moments more space to lead to the next moment I have learned that there are just so many more ways things can go than I can imagine. So many beautiful ideas have blossomed over the years because I stopped myself from jumping in, because I quietly asked myself, "what if?" instead of speaking. Apparently my opinions aren't often necessary for the lives around me to unfold beautifully.

Being attentive to my thoughts and words also means that I can be selective in what I share—meaning just the really good stuff. That has allowed me to keep my two cents much more often, and I feel richer for it! That's not to say that I actively avoid conversation—people ask my thoughts, and conversations with my kids have been known to lead to bouncing excitement as we share our thoughts and opinions about many things. But it is specifically in those moments when people are receptive to others' ideas: when they seek them out. When they are connected to a larger conversation.

Think about it for a moment. How much fun is it to have people tossing their opinions at you when you haven't asked for them? Not very. Unsolicited advice? Usually annoying. Why? Because it doesn't match where your thoughts are—it is more distracting than anything. Your best chance in being relevant and helpful to anyone, child or adult, is when you're responding to *their* thoughts and questions, joining them where *they* are, not indiscriminately sharing every thought you have. Take that mindful moment to evaluate whether the thought that just occurred to you is worth sharing, worth the effort the listener will need to make to move from where their thoughts are currently to connect this new one you've shared so it makes sense in their perspective.

Another helpful reason to strive for an attentive state of mind is to keep an eye out for our unthinking reactions. Those voices from the past in our head, spouting edicts and judging our actions harshly, can definitely affect our mood and our actions. Or those habits we've formed over the years that may not be serving us as well any more. Or fear which immediately sends our pulse racing and words tumbling out, yet we're not sure why. Rather than let autopilot take over and respond in our habitual ways, these are moments that would be great to catch so we can re-consider the situation and choose our response to this moment based on our new perspective. What once was a knee-jerk reaction can become a choice.

What living mindfully helps us do is recognize the many choices available to us every day. If we don't see any choices, we feel trapped. We feel like we don't have control of our lives. Our days are an endless procession of telling ourselves we have to do this and that with no end in sight. We lash out thoughtlessly, in general frustration.

Yet when we realize that everything we do is a choice suddenly we feel free, breathing is easier, and a smile is within easy reach—even while changing our young child's diaper for the gazillionth time. There are so many choices in there! If we take the diaper example, you could choose to not change it right now, leaving it for a while longer. What might happen? Maybe your spouse gets home soon and changes it. If not, eventually your child will probably become uncomfortable wearing it, maybe developing a rash; maybe not. Would that be frustrating for your child, and even more a challenge for you to deal with in the end? You might choose to just wait a little while. Or you could remove the diaper and leave your child running free for a while. Maybe they'd have an accident—how hard would that to clean up versus a diaper change? Maybe you guys could play in the backyard while going diaper free, making clean up even easier. Or maybe your child has a really messy diaper right now and outside would be an easier, and more fun, way to clean it all up: a couple buckets of warm, soapy water and sponges for you both to play with.

Maybe one of those options sounds perfect for the moment you're in! Or maybe they all sound like more work right now and a regular ol' quickie diaper change sounds right. But now it's not being foisted upon you and out of your control—you're *choosing* the circumstances of the diaper change. And now there are even more choices. In this moment, would it be easier to take your child to your regular changing spot or to grab the essentials and bring them to your child?

For me, taking a moment to realize I have many options, even with the most mundane activities, and then mindfully choosing which one best suits the current circumstances, helps shift me out of any frustration I was initially feeling because now I remember the reasons *why* I'm making that choice. And, unsurprisingly, when I approach the diaper change (or whatever situation I initially felt trapped by) mindfully and with minimal frustration it usually goes that much more smoothly—even if my child gets frustrated in the moment I don't react back, spiraling us deeper. When we are careful and considerate with our thoughts we see so many more options to a given situation and soon we realize we have and make a lot more choices than we often give ourselves credit for.

We control our lives—not the other way around.

Living mindfully is not only incredibly supportive of an unschooling environment, it has grown to become a wonderful perspective from which to approach my life in general. With both my actions and my relationships, with both children and adults, being fully attentive to the situation at hand, taking a moment to discover and consider the choices available, and moving forward respectfully from there, continues to bring me a level of peace and compassion that had eluded me earlier.

Finding Joy

What do I mean by the word joy? Certainly it means happiness, pleasure. Most people can find happiness in response to good things that happen to them or around them. Yet when disappointing things happen, they are thrown into despair. It's tough to be at the mercy of outside events!

What I'd like to talk about is the deeper sense of joy that I found developed alongside my growing understanding of unschooling. It's a sense of self that no longer seems quite so susceptible to the whims of life and luck. That's important because a joyful life is not without problems or strains or challenges.

I thought I'd share a few of the insights that have helped me over the years to find joy more often. This process was, and continues to be, about perspective—discovering new ways to look at life. My life experiences make me uniquely me, which is different from you, yet I share them because you may find something helpful to toss around as part of *your* journey to living joyfully with unschooling.

One helpful realization I've had as part of moving to unschooling has been that being right is overrated. Growing up a "good" student—that was a hard one for me to shake! But the world really isn't as black and white as we were led to believe. Doing *something* is usually better than doing nothing. When you're exploring yourself and how you dance with the world, instead of feeling paralyzed by the search for the "right" answer, think it through and go with your gut—try it out! You know what? Even if you're "wrong" (wrong only in the sense that you change your mind later), the quickest and most effective way to learn whether something makes sense to you is to live with it for a while and see how it plays out. Gain more life experience with it. Make choices. Learn. Incorporate your experiences and make more choices. Life is a process. And there's nothing wrong with quitting stuff.

Another big mind-shift that played a part in finding joy more often was to stop giving the responsibility for my happiness to others. Moving to unschooling asks us to take responsibility for more and more pieces of our lives, to shift from doing what is expected of us, to making our own choices. Once I took ownership of my own happiness I stopped looking for it outside of myself. Looking inside is where it's under my control, where I can make choices and take action. Instead of being at the mercy of things happening around me, instead of my emotions and mood being mostly a response to outside influences, I began choosing how I felt.

At first I worried that this might put distance between myself and others but, playing around with it, the really interesting thing I discovered was that just because I didn't take on others' emotions, didn't mean I ignored them. In fact, it turned out that I could sit *more* comfortably with them. Taking them on myself had been adding another layer, or filter, through which I saw the situation. When I stopped doing that, I found I could see their perspective of the situation more clearly and easily: I had *more* empathy, not less.

A third insight that grew from my shift to unschooling was an accompanying shift in my time frame. As I changed my perspective on learning from compulsory school years to lifelong learning, I also began looking beyond the immediate impact of moments to the bigger picture. I could be in the moment, *and* realize that in the grand scheme of things, most things aren't as dire as they may appear. My perspective shifted. I found I could be more present with both happiness and disappointment in those moments, but they no longer took me on an internal roller coaster ride because I didn't equate the longer-term deep sense of joy I felt inside with the emotions of the moments I was in.

Another really helpful realization grew out of that shift to a longer-term perspective: I will always be learning. This always hits home when I look back at myself five and ten years earlier. I see how my understanding of things has changed and grown, yet I also refuse to think of my younger selves as "wrong"—I was doing my best at the time, thinking and evaluating and making the best choices I could in the moment.

Projecting that forward, I also realize that in ten years I may well look back at my perspective today and see it as inexperienced and incomplete: "If I knew then what I know now." But we don't. And we won't. And any angst and fear about the future that I let wreak havoc in the present only clouds my judgment. Instead, I choose to be kind to present-day me and to look forward with wonder, anticipating the experiences that will help me discover new things about the world, about me, about my family, and how we will swirl through life in the years ahead.

So as I continue exploring who I am, comfortable with the idea that I will always be learning, I only ask that I stay true to myself in each moment. That I continue walking towards the person I want to be. And my journey to unschooling has played a huge role in getting me to a place where I am comfortable with the person I am *and* with the idea that I will continue to learn and grow and change. And that's a joyful place to be.

appendix

"I Can Read, You Know!"

"I can read, you know!" my nine year-old daughter retorted lightly to her older brother this past summer. I don't even remember what he had said to her, but her reply stood out. It was a turning point for her, to declare that she could read.

I had taken my three kids out of school just over a year before that incident. Or, more rightly, they had jumped at the chance to leave when it was offered to them! At the time, my daughter was in grade two and one of her teacher's favourite students. She did well and seemed to enjoy going to school, though she was in one of the lower reading groups. I was therefore surprised, albeit happily, that she was on cloud nine for the next three days contemplating the fact she did not have to return to school when March Break was over.

Although she had read the early readers they sent home from school without much complaint, she did not want to pick up a book once home. She could often be heard to declare "I can't read" and nothing I said would convince her otherwise. I told her that if she was interested in reading a book herself, she could just ask me any words she came across that she didn't know yet and I'd tell her. No thanks, was her reply.

So I completely let it go; no pressure or expectations. At the same time I made a point of reading books to her and her brothers just about every day. Her older brother had been given the first Harry Potter book, so we started there. Everyone enjoyed the story immensely and we soon worked our way through all four books numerous times, eagerly anticipated the release of the fifth book in June, and then powered through it together in three days. If a movie we watched was based on a book, I might mention it. If someone asked a question that needed to be looked up in a book, I just did it. Books were just another part of our lives; I didn't make a big deal out of it. And whenever she asked, I read for her. Or her older brother would, usually when they were playing video games. I mentioned to her in passing that I was still coming across new words, that nobody knows them all ... and it probably helped for her to see me stumble trying to pronounce new words and names in the Harry Potter books.

Once in a while she would read a word or two, here and there. Occasionally I pointed this out to her, but still she insisted she couldn't read. It seemed her definition of "being able to read" was being able to read the Harry Potter books fluently. Or, more generally I think, being able to read and understand "real" books—those at the level of her vocabulary, understanding and interest—not the early readers where the story often suffers severely at the hands of limited vocabulary in the name of being "able to read". Sound reasoning, I think now. What's the rush?

Our first year of unschooled learning passed this way. I could see snatches though. As always with natural learning, the moments came unexpectedly and then moved on. It's when you put them all together over a period of time that you can start to see the picture coming alive on the canvas. On drives she started commenting on signs. Interesting. And reading stuff from TV commercials. Very interesting.

And then, seemingly out of the blue this past summer, her comment to her brother: "I can read, you know!" It may not seem like much, but I felt like she had turned a corner. Even though she had not yet picked up a book, even though she still openly declared she "hated books", in her mind it was no longer about her "being a reader"; it was about her being interested in reading.

I had been reading the Harry Potter books to the kids over and over the past year and we finally got them on CD in mid-summer. The boys had had their fill but she would cozy up in her room and listen to them regularly. Sometimes I would bring her food, or tea and she'd smile and say thanks and continue listening.

September came and after listening to all five a number of times she started writing down things that were interesting to her: Umbridge's speech, the prophecy, the

Sphinx's riddle, listing the names of the centaurs, clues she found that matched up with other books etc. I noticed her notebook filling up and one night while I was out I picked her up a new one I thought she'd like. She really appreciated that and she used it for her "good copies"—she said sometimes she's writing so fast it's hard to read.

This writing led to her looking things up in the books since at times she couldn't quite figure out the words from the CDs.

She took all five books up to her room and placed them beside the CD player so she had quick access. Not long after that she mentioned that she was sometimes following along in the book while listening. I thought that was cool.

Then one afternoon a few days later she came down from her room to show me that she had read the first two chapters of Philosopher's Stone! And said she was very surprised that the words aren't nearly as hard as she remembers (I imagine from looking at the books when I first started reading them). And she pointed out that many of the words in the Harry Potter books are harder to read since they are made up words that she doesn't see elsewhere. Cool! The next morning she spent in bed reading and made it to chapter four. She was very pleased with herself. For the next few days she read in bed every morning and at various times during the day and night. One night she brought her heating blanket in the backyard to the swing, ran the extension cord, brought out her pillows and a flashlight and settled in to read ... until it started to rain! She was so excited; she brought the book everywhere and was constantly saying, "I want to read" and finding a quiet place. And I quietly found a moment here and there to sneak away and find where she was holed up to catch a glimpse of her engrossed in a book.

Throughout October she was still going full steam ahead on her reading and writing—she was immersing herself in words. It hadn't taken her long to finish reading Philosopher's Stone and she soon started Chamber of Secrets but after a few chapters said it was pretty boring because she knew it all. She said at least while she's listening to the audio books she gets to do other things. And boy, does she do other things! Hmmm, let's see if I can list some of them: sewing costumes for her stuffed animals; sewing pillows for sale; creating wire jewelry using beads she's found around the house and designing and creating her own clasps; repairing couch pillows, pajamas, and Christmas stockings. Then she moved on to more writing—she marked all her favourite places in the books and wrote out many of the signs, letters, songs etc. that she could find in the storyline. Sometimes she wrote them by hand, sometimes she typed them. Some are hung on her door, others placed in vignettes around her room, and still others stored safely for use as props at the Live and Learn conference talent show this summer. More playing with words.

In November she pulled out our Magical Worlds of Harry Potter book and for the next few days she read that regularly. Gently stepping beyond the Harry Potter books themselves to one that would likely have the same vocabulary she was already comfortable with; and feeding her passion at the same time. Now and then she read some passages aloud to me and at other times she would explain what she had read. Then a couple weeks later she was reading all her email from her conference friends. Up until that point she had always asked me to read them to her. Then she took a Nancy Drew book from our library at home and started reading it. She was now definitely getting more comfortable with her reading and expanding beyond her initial "Harry Potter" zone.

I find it so interesting to follow her path to reading, which began in school with early readers. But she rejected those books once she came home to learn. She made no attempt at reading on her own over the next year and a half, but did lots of listening to the Harry Potter series and a few other books I read to them. Then a breakthrough when she declared that she could read, shifting the focus from being a reader to being interested in reading. Finding a passionate interest she, within the course of a month, whizzed through the stages of writing things out as she listened to the audio books, looking things up in the books, following along in the books, and then reading one of the books independently. I'm so grateful that unschooling allowed her to find her own path to reading.

And a couple of weeks ago we were chatting in the kitchen and she asked about a book of names we have and then exclaimed in mock horror "Arghh! I'm turning into a bookworm!"

First published in: *Life Learning Magazine*, May/June 2004

Everything I Need to Know I Learned

from Video Games

"He'd play video games all day if I let him," you confide in your neighbour and she nods her head in sympathy. "That can't be good, right?"

As life learners we strive to give our children the freedom to pursue their interests and passions. We see that they learn quickly and happily—almost effortlessly—when they are caught up in and enjoying what they are doing. It's pretty easy to let it flow when you feel their interests are worthwhile, but what if you have a hard time seeing the value in what they choose to pursue? Do you catch your breath and eventually demand they move on to something else?

Gaming is often an area of interest where many people have a hard time seeing the value. When I realized that playing video games was a deep, passionate interest for my now 12-year-old son Joseph I decided to take an active role. Instead of limiting his playing time in hopes that he would find something "better" to do, I fully supported his interest. I spent time watching him play, chatting with him, I tried it out myself, I helped him find information he wanted. It didn't take me long to realize that he was constantly learning new things. Here's what I found, along with some ideas on how you can support and get involved with your child's interest in video games.

Let's look at reading. Joseph was almost ten when we began unschooling. In school he had struggled to finish assigned early chapter books, but at home in the evenings he devoured 80-page computer printouts of game walkthroughs. With school out of the way he has continued to read game information voraciously—with the occasional fiction book along the way.

In fact, video games may well spark an interest in learning to read. Children may see it as their first real purpose for reading. It has been that way for our seven-year-old son—he has been reading game play words for quite a while now. Many games, especially RPGs (role-playing games), have a rich story environment. Spend time with your child and read the text so they can enjoy and appreciate the storyline, not just the action. It's like reading an animated storybook!

At some point they will progress past the level where we're any help— either with skill or suggestions. It's time for some research! Getting a magazine subscription for the applicable game system is very helpful. They'll get articles on upcoming games and abbreviated walkthroughs, often with visual screenshots. Player's guides are great—

beautiful art work and answers to just about any question they may have.

And don't forget about the internet. At first Joseph would ask us to find things for him—guides and FAQs (frequently asked questions) about the game he was playing. But over the last year he has taken to doing this himself. He learned quickly that when searching the internet spelling counts! Now he also finds fan sites and evaluates their reliability based on his knowledge of the game. These skills develop naturally because they want information to help them accomplish something in their game, but they are applicable to any research they do in the future.

And over the last few months he's discovered message boards. Here you can read conversations between players. It may take a bit more weeding out of extraneous information to get to his answer (another useful skill), but it's worthwhile nonetheless. And if he doesn't find what he's looking for he can post his question directly.

This level of research can in turn lead to meaningful writing. They may be interested in writing comments to the gaming magazine they read regularly. As they get comfortable on the gaming message boards they may not only post their questions but begin to answer the questions of others. They may be interested in writing their own walkthroughs and FAQs. This is *real* writing.

While researching games Joseph discovered a fan fiction website. Here writers post stories based on characters and/or situations from video games, books, movies, and so on. When he noticed his ten-year-old sister writing stories based on her passionate interest in Harry Potter he passed the site along to her and she has spent many hours reading there as well as writing. Last I heard her current story was over 30,000 words long. I smiled. Things flow very nicely when I don't try to change the course.

Typing is another useful skill Joseph's picked up along the way. He's never been interested in writing by hand, nor in typical "learn-to-type" software. But when he expressed an interest in online gaming we set him up, got him a keyboard and within two weeks he was typing well! When we asked if he was enjoying it he said it was a dream come true. He had finally found a community of players with comparable levels of interest and gaming skills.

Next let's look at math. Typically there is a time component and some form of money. There is also monitoring your characters' health and level, and anticipating damage and experience points to figure out your chances of surviving upcoming battles and leveling up. Not to mention all the money conversations you'll have with them as they save up to purchase new games, bargain hunt for used games, or place bids on eBay auctions! The opportunities to play with numbers are endless.

There is also plenty of logic in game play. Many side quests require puzzles to be solved to get useful items or even to continue to the next level. There's logic in the approach to boss battles, determining weak areas and choosing attacks that take full advantage. There are often mazes to be solved as you move through levels.

Even higher level math comes up regularly. One evening when Joseph was 11 he asked me to help him figure out an algebraic formula with two variables from one of his games: $(Y / 5) + X$. This is an aspect of the game he is just getting into this time around. We discussed the formula and went through the examples they gave in the player's guide. We talked about rounding. Later I passed him in the hall and he said, "They sure do build up their levels slowly!" You just know he had been pondering the formula and trying out various combinations.

I have seen pages and pages of percentage charts in player's guides. By using these charts a player can build up skill in the classes and parameters they prefer, creating their own unique characters and ensuring a well-balanced party. I've seen Joseph pouring over them in deep concentration. In fact, when he was studying the charts for *Golden Sun 2* he remarked that they were the most important part of the player's guide. These statistical charts had six attributes that changed individually based on, from what I could tell, three independent variables for, on average, five possible subclasses. And there were 25 of these charts—one for each of the default classes plus combinations of classes to create complex classes. Whew.

There is so much going on in video games that you can discuss—it's like critiquing a book or a movie. We've had many discussions about storylines. Discussions about characters and how they develop. The music (some games are fully orchestrated with original soundtracks) and how it helps build the mood. The art (Joseph has created some really beautiful character sketches) and technical advances in graphics. What's the climax of the game and how is everything resolved? Or is it?

Joseph commented to me a few months ago that what he loves about video games is a really deep story. Games without deep stories make him bored. Fast. Books allow you to read a great story and imagine it. Movies take it another step and bring in the visual element. Video games take it yet another step and allow you to interact with the story. In many games how you interact with the story determines the twists and turns the plot will take. The replay value is amazing because you can play it multiples times, often times through the eyes of different characters, and learning different bits of the story each time.

He has come to realize that his passion is not really video games per se, but video games as a medium to immersion in a great, deep story. If I had limited his playing time and not helped him pursue this interest, I don't think he would have realized this. And I would have been too busy trying to get him to do other "more worthy" things to see it myself. Now I realize that it would have been like me limiting the time he was allowed to read each day. It seems a little ridiculous when I think about it that way.

Gamers also learn many things from the game story-line itself. Joseph has developed a great interest in mythology. One summer evening last year we were all sitting around the campfire and I started reading excerpts from *The Magical Worlds of Harry Potter* by David Colbert out loud. Well, the mythology Joseph knew and related to what we were reading was phenomenal! He would often finish the sentence I was reading. And he would connect it back to some of the games he enjoys playing. And he would connect the games to each other. Even though the games themselves weren't related, they were all drawing on the same mythological stories as their basis, or as a meaningful basis for naming characters and moves. It was a really fun night!

And lest you think that cheats are for cheaters, let's take a quick look at them. When you think of how most games are designed, you realize there are a number of variables that the player needs keep track of—like health, current location/map, weapons, enemy type/weaknesses etc. The player needs to be on top of all these things to successfully navigate the game. What a cheat often does is basically fix one of these variables so the player no longer needs to worry about it—he can concentrate on mastering the others. For example, a cheat may give you infinite health. At first you think, "What a waste, where's the challenge then?" but look a bit further. Now they can concentrate on say, learning their way around the level using the map, or practicing battles with their weaker weapons to improve their skills. And they learn that sometimes fixing one variable has unexpected consequences.

Other cheats bring the object-oriented code to life. In *The Legend of Zelda: Ocarina of Time* there are cheats so that you can change the colour of Link's tunic and his size. Simple and meaningless you think. But no—they will likely notice that his tunic colour has changed even in the game introduction, not just the game itself. How when they enlarge Link he is bigger than the gate, even the building, but he still cannot enter when it's locked. How he doesn't look like he's moving when he steps because although he takes up most of the screen the code for walking still moves him the same distance.

And in *The Simpsons Hit & Run* there is a cheat so the car will bounce. "What on earth for?!" you think. But playing around with it you discover something interesting. When you bounce high over the houses near the edge of the level, you can see behind them. There is nothing there. You have reached the end of the code. The designers never imagined that a user would be able to see past the houses, so they didn't bother adding anything. It is just empty space. Interesting!

These cheats make the code come alive before their eyes. They begin to understand how code works. They may not be able to explain it, but they intuitively understand it. And if in the course of their lives it comes up, they'll understand the technical terms immediately because they have seen it in action. It will connect to their gaming experience and have meaning. I will never look at cheats the same way again.

Now that they've played around with the games themselves young people may be interested in learning about programming—either web site development or even game programming itself. Joseph spent some time learning about web site content and development when creating a fan site. It's a great place to start because there are a number of tools around that don't require a lot of programming knowledge.

He has also developed an interest in game design. We picked up *RPG Maker II* along with the guide for Joseph last Christmas and he has spent many hours with it. It is not for the faint of heart though. The guide reads like a computer manual but he loves it and each time he makes a major discovery he starts up a new game to put it to full use. I'm lucky enough to be his official game tester!

Many people believe that gaming is a passive pastime, but in reality, though it is obviously not physically active (until you try the Eyetoy!), it is mentally challenging and engaging. James Paul Gee, a reading professor in the School of Education at the University of Wisconsin-Madison, believes "Learning isn't about memorizing isolated facts. It's about connecting and manipulating them." (*Wired*, May 2003, High Score Education: Games, not school, are teaching kids to think) A great game skirts the edge of the players' level of competence, each new level pushing them to the limit of what they can do, enticing them to learn more. They are immersed in the game world and experience the flow of all their attention being powerfully focused—their mind working quickly making the connections needed to meet the game's challenges. After spending many hours with his students immersed in video games Gee concluded that "Young gamers today aren't training to be gun-toting carjackers. They're learning how to learn." I see it every day.

Seymour Papert, author of *The Connected Family: Bridging the Digital Generation Gap*, recognizes that "talking about games and learning is an important activity" and "encourages parents to engage in conversations with their kids about learning" (*Game Developer*, June 1998, Does Easy Do It? Children, Games, and Learning). That's not a tall order for life learning families!

I am always astonished when I look at the many different places Joseph's interest in video games has taken him. The many things he has learned along the way. And to extend it further, I think this approach is wonderful for any parent whose child has a deep, passionate interest. Whether it is trains, collectible cards, video games or Harry Potter, take a few slow, deep breaths and help them fully explore their passion—you'll be amazed at where the journey will take you!

First published in: *Life Learning Magazine*, Sept/Oct 2004

thank you!

Thanks for inviting me along on your unschooling journey. I hope you've found this book to be a joyful companion.

I wish you and your family all the best as you continue to live and learn!

Learning freely, living joyfully.

acknowledgments

Huge thanks to Alex Peace, my editor, for her always wonderful eye, clear proofreading, and sparkling conversation.

And to Jane Dixon-Smith, at JD Smith Design, for the great book cover design.

I also want to thank my blog readers! Their thoughtful feedback and comments extend the conversation, and always keep me thinking. I love thinking.

And I continue to be grateful to my family, for their love, support, and unwavering curiosity about the world around us.

They are my inspiration.

about Pam Laricchia

It has always been Pam's nature to question things that didn't make sense, but somehow it didn't occur to her to question the education system as her eldest reached school age. Until it just wasn't working for her son.

In her quest to find a learning environment where her children would thrive, she eventually came across the idea of homeschooling and was thrilled to discover it was legal in Canada. A few weeks later the children were home from school for March Break and they just didn't go back. They were ecstatic with their newly found playtime and she was happily researching homeschooling.

A couple more weeks and she came across the idea of unschooling, and after a few months of deschooling that's where they landed. She has been happily unschooling her three children since 2002, when they were ages ten, eight, and five.

Watching her children explore their interests and passions has been an incredible learning experience in itself, one she is excited to share with others through her writing and speaking.

Other books

Free to Learn: Five Ideas for a Joyful Unschooling Life

Pam shares the five paradigm-changing ideas about learning and living that freed her family from the school schedule: real learning, following interests, making choices, why not yes, and living together. These ideas were, and still are, key to our unschooling lives.

Free to Live: Create a Thriving Unschooling Home

Pam discusses the four characteristics that have had the most positive impact on their unschooling lifestyle: curiosity, patience, strong relationships, and trust. Understanding why these characteristics are so helpful makes it easier for parents to choose to respond in ways that support unschooling, rather than undermine it.

Find her writing online: livingjoyfully.ca

At Pam's website you can sign up to receive *Exploring Unschooling*, her free email series that serves as a helpful introduction to unschooling. You'll also find her blog, her twice-monthly newsletter, and the various articles she's had published over the years.

Made in the USA
Coppell, TX
23 January 2024

28126152R00177